MW01092465

PIRATES & SMUGGLERS
—— *of the* ——
TREASURE COAST

Patrick S. Mesmer & Patricia Mesmer

THE
History
PRESS

Published by The History Press
Charleston, SC
www.historypress.com

First published 2019

Manufactured in the United States

ISBN 9781467141796

Library of Congress Control Number: 2019945078

Notice: The information in this book is true and complete to the best of our knowledge. It is offered without guarantee on the part of the authors or The History Press. The authors and The History Press disclaim all liability in connection with the use of this book.

This book is dedicated to the following people:
To our loving parents who brought us into this amazing life,
Terry, Hal and Corky.
To the pirates and all other like-minded people who believe in what we do.
And to our fellow residents of the Treasure Coast of Florida who want to keep
it a magical place by preserving its history, folklore and natural beauty through
conservation and common sense.

Gator! *Sketch by Don Maitz.*

Contents

Preface   11
Introduction   13

1. The Ancient Residents   19
   Florida's First Pirates   21
   Pedro Menéndez de Avilés, 1565   22
   Terrifying Story, 1570   24
   Jonathan Dickinson, 1696   25
   Ais Treasure   27

2. The Treasure Coast Is Born   30
   Turmoil in Europe   32
   Spanish Conquest   35
   The 1715 Fleet Begins the Journey   36
   Salvage   39

3. The Golden Age of Piracy   41
   The Allure of the Lifestyle   41
   Captain Henry Jennings—Pirate or Privateer?   44
   Charles Vane   48
   Black Sam Bellamy   51
   Mary Hallet—The Sea Witch of Billingsgate   52
   Palmar De Ays   53
   The Most Infamous Edward Teach—Blackbeard   55

Contents

4. Don Pedro Gibert   60
   A Wild, Untamed Land   60
   Son of the Sea   62
   Dead Cats Don't Mew—You Know What to Do   63
   Fugitives from the Law   65
   The Sensational Trial   66

5. Smuggling and the Slave Trade   70
   Latecomers to Florida   70
   The First Seminole War, 1817–18   72
   The Second Seminole War, 1835–42   73
   The Third Seminole War, 1855–58   75
   Outside Aid for the Seminoles   76
   Encounter at Jupiter, Florida   77
   Jesup's Pleas for War's End   78
   Slave Trade Act of 1808   79
   Journey of Misery   80
   Black Seminoles   82
   The Search for Help on Andros Island   83
   Red Bays   84

6. Smuggling on the Treasure Coast, 1845–65   86
   The Civil War Comes to South Florida's East Coast   89
   USS *Roebuck*   92
   USS *Union*   94
   USS *Sagamore*   94

7. Florida's Whiskey Pirates and Smugglers   96
   The Great Florida Land Boom   96
   Temperance Comes to Florida   98
   Wild Times Indeed   100
   The Real McCoy   103
   Folk Hero   109
   Marie Waite, "Spanish Marie"   109
   Gertrude "Cleo" Lythgoe   110
   "Big Al" in Jupiter   112

CONTENTS

8. The Notorious Ashley Gang   114
   Bank Robbers   118
   Bootleggers   121
   The Real Story   127
   Aftermath   127

9. The Drug Trade on the Treasure Coast, 1960–Present   129
   Smuggling "Mary Jane"   130
   Treasure Coast, Smuggler's Paradise   131
   Smuggling in the Air   132
   A Never-Ending Battle   133
   The Boat Business Soars   133
   Buried Treasure on the Treasure Coast   134
   Successful Smuggler Turned "Rat"   135
   A Fisherman's Brush with the Law   136

10. Pirates and Smugglers of the Treasure Coast Today   139
    Treasure Island   141
    The Real Pirates of the Caribbean   141
    Captain Bob   144
    Blackbeard Lives   146
    Captain Dan Leeward and Holly Roger   148
    Don Maitz   149
    Captain Fizz   151
    Captain Honey Badger   152
    Commodore Cutter   153

Conclusion   155
Bibliography   157
About the Authors   159

The coast of Florida was long the favorite resort, and her bays and inlets, but little is known to the rest of the world, long continued to be the safe retreat of the bold, desperate, and reckless race of beings, who, during the seventeenth century, so much infested in the southern seas. It was from this coast that they drew their main supplies; and when driven from the ocean, it was here in these unknown regions that they sought safety. And according to tradition, it was to the Spanish forts and settlements along the coast that they carried much of the blood-stained wealth, which they had gathered by piracy from the four corners of the earth.

—*Jacob Rhett Motte,* Journey into the Wilderness, *1845*

Preface

I have always had a passion for the study of history and the charismatic people who created it, especially those who lived their lives on what I consider "the edge." People like Bill McCoy, John Ashley, Gertrude Lythgoe and Edward Teach existed among us with a seemingly endless zeal for adventure and danger. Throughout the pages of the past, their stories always seem to shine brighter than all the others. I see each of them as a real person, like you or me, who, at some great crossroads in their lives, was faced with a monumental decision to either choose the common, safe road or take the far riskier path that would propel them into the realm of the immortal. The latter would cause them to burn bright, like a meteor, for a short time, and then burn out quickly, leaving a lasting impression on our psyches that would never die. These men and women refused to be tamed and lived their lives by their own rules until they met their end. Our society chooses to view these qualities as either truly admirable or detestable but always looks on them from afar with objective, child-like fascination. We love to search for greatness in others despite their flaws or methods; it is in our nature.

I have always been fascinated with many controversial historical figures, especially infamous criminals like the gangsters of the 1920s. When I first read the stories about Al Capone, "Lucky" Luciano, Meyer Lansky and Carlo Gambino, I was immediately intrigued. I learned that often these men were products of extremely tough environments and upbringings. Most were immigrants of Italian or Irish descent who, upon their arrival to their new home in the United States, faced terrible prejudice and persecution due to their cultural diversity and ethnicity. Even though I was shocked at the level of violence and intimidation they were capable of, I also noted the fact that they banded together to form what would become the most powerful and feared crime syndicates of all time. Despite the viciousness and illegal nature of their activities, I admired the "bonds of secrecy" and loyalty that the early Mafia families had to one another. To me, true power is in commitment, decisive actions rather than words and strength in numbers.

As a young person, I became obsessed with the subject of piracy. When Disney's "Pirates of the Caribbean" artwork and theme park ride came out, I was hooked. I began to seek out books and short stories relating to the buccaneers of the sixteenth and seventeenth centuries. To my young and impressionable mind, there was something irresistible about the idea of being free and wild on the high seas with no rules. Men like Edward Teach (Blackbeard) ruled not by killing people at every turn but by fear and intimidation. When I think of larger-than-life characters like Blackbeard, I try to separate the myriad of pirate clichés that riddle our culture and imagine what the real man was like. Teach knew that it was better if a potential prize ship gave up in terror before a costly sea battle ever occurred. To me, this is one of the reasons he was so successful. He had to be a true leader of men, a diplomat, a fair disciplinarian and a vicious warrior, as well as an expert sailor and navigator. He also had to consistently lead his men to profitable prizes, or they could possibly turn on him. Edward Teach must have been a truly amazing character.

The place in which we live, Florida's Treasure Coast, has a rich history of smuggling and piracy. In 2016, my wife, Tricia, and I were approached by The History Press to write a book that documents the legends and paranormal activity of many of the region's locations. This publication is called *Ghosts of the Treasure Coast*, and it has proven to be very popular in this area. We have run a successful business for many years called Port Salerno Ghost Tours. When the publisher offered to work with us on a new project, I suggested this book on the subjects that are very near and dear to me. Tricia and I are very excited to present this work to you and hope that you come visit us and take one of our tours. We sincerely hope that you enjoy *Pirates and Smugglers of the Treasure Coast*.

Introduction

A Tradition of Piracy and Smuggling

I t's around noon on a Saturday afternoon, and I'm driving north along the ten-mile stretch of Indian River Drive that runs adjacent to the Intracoastal Waterway. This is the route I always take whenever I go to Fort Pierce, Florida, for business. It's my belief that it is one of the most beautiful roadways in the country. When I pass the Fort Pierce city limit sign, I start looking ahead along the left side of the narrow road. The small sign is there; "Old Fort Park," so I slow down to turn in. This is one of the most special spots in all of Florida. The place is a gem, a wonderful little historical site surrounded by great sprawling oaks. I park my truck and get out, pausing for a moment to take in a deep breath of air that is thick with the scent with the sea. There is something soothing about this place; maybe it's the sound of the wind rustling through the giant oak trees in the yard or the gentle rhythm of the waves on the beach a short distance away. I walk out onto the grass, past the largest of the oaks, and pause to gaze at the large mound in front of me. I know a little of the history of this place, so I take a moment to run it through my mind like an old, cherished song.

I have always been in awe of all places of significant historical importance, and this site is no exception. Before me is an original burial mound of the ancient people who resided here before my ancestors of European descent ever considered traveling across the great pond to find a new life. I approach the rise and walk up the crude stairway fashioned from small, flat concrete slabs to the top of the mound. After taking in the magnificent view of the river, I close my eyes and concentrate, letting my mind wander back hundreds of years, and try to imagine what this place was like when the native people ruled this place. I know, from my studies, that the Ais were not only strong, rebellious warriors, but a deeply spiritual people as well. From the strange sensation of contentment and wonder I am experiencing, it's not hard for me to believe that there is something very special about this site.

This place is also the site of the original Fort Pierce, a crude outpost consisting of a cluster of palmetto log blockhouses placed here in the early 1800s during the Second Seminole War to aid in the fight against the tough, resilient Seminole people. One of the commanders of this fort was a young William Tecumseh Sherman, fresh out of West Point. In his memoirs, he states how much he loved the place during his tenure there. Sherman valued his solitude and loved the outdoors, so the lonely duty in Fort Pierce suited him. He even had a pet deer that he domesticated and allowed into his quarters. The great Seminole war chief Wildcat, or Coacoochie to his people, surrendered to Sherman very close to this spot. The fort was built on the north side of the great Ais mound and was in service throughout the war. It seems ironic that the military outpost is gone without a trace, but the mound remains.

I let these events replay through my mind as the cool breeze rifles through my clothes. I hear a rustle in the tree's branches and notice that a red-shouldered hawk has just landed on one of the high branches. He glares at me with his intense, black eyes, as if sharing my thoughts of the ancient ones.

One of the reasons that I love Florida so dearly is the dark treasure-trove of history that surrounds it. Its tragic history is a torrid blend of betrayal, greed and violence. Florida's history is a subject I find so compelling that I simply cannot look away. I especially love the Treasure Coast, an area of the eastern coast of the state that stretches from Sebastian Inlet to Jupiter Inlet. It is still very beautiful, although it is hard to imagine what it must have been like before the hordes of people, condos, houses, paved roads and industry moved in. Every few years, Mother Nature reminds us of her vast power by conjuring up one of her violent hellfire storms that descends on us with a vengeance, sometimes smashing us with so much brutal force that our very coastline is altered. It is during these times that we residents of the Treasure Coast remember that the pristine seacoast is like a fickle lover—both beautiful and cruel. Maybe it's the climate that keeps us content. Though unbearably hot and inhospitable in the summer months, our winters compensate with a delightfully temperate climate that is the envy of the entire country.

Fort Pierce mound. *Photo by author*.

Where did the Treasure Coast get its name? The term was coined by John J. Schumann Jr. and Harry J. Schultz of the *Vero Beach Press Journal* shortly after salvagers began recovering Spanish treasure off the coast in 1961. The discovery of treasure from the 1715 Treasure Fleet, lost in a hurricane near the Sebastian Inlet, was of major historical importance and brought international attention to the area. In the 1950s, a building contractor named Kip Wagner began finding Spanish coins on the beach. Contrary to the beliefs of several experts, Kip suspected that a major Spanish treasure flotilla consisting of eleven ships was hit by a terrible hurricane and wrecked on the beaches of what are now known as Indian River and St. Lucie Counties. Historians of the time knew about the 1715 wrecks, but the consensus was that the disaster occurred hundreds of miles to the south, near the Marquesas. Not only did Kip Wagner believe that the wrecks occurred far north of where the experts said they were located, but he was also confident that one of the wreck sites was right out in the short surf just south of Sebastian Inlet. Through hard work and perseverance, Kip and his Reale Eight Company made the discovery, confirming his research and making him famous. He would also learn valuable lessons about salvage rights, as many interlopers tried to move in on his sites. Aware of the magnitude of his discovery, Kip brought in a partner, Mel Fisher, who owned a successful dive shop in California. Fisher would end up taking over the entire salvage operation, successfully locating many of the 1715 wreck sites. He would later move his operation south, eventually locating the wreck of the *Atocha* southwest of the Florida Keys. This wreck's $400 million horde of gold, silver, emeralds and priceless artifacts made Mel Fisher a household name.

Back to my sightseeing journey. I thank the native spirits for allowing me to share in the sacred beauty of the Fort Pierce Mound and head back south along Indian River Drive. I soon come to the Jensen Beach Causeway and cross over to South Hutchinson Island, a long, thin strip of barrier island that stretches from Fort Pierce to Stuart, Florida. Traveling south, I see the Elliott Museum on my left, a wonderful center of art and technology, as well as the home of over ninety classic automobiles collected by prolific inventor Sterling Elliott in the early twentieth century. I could spend the whole day in this museum, so I reluctantly drive past it, making a mental note myself to come back later when I have more time.

I soon arrive at my destination, which is the most well-known historical site in the area: Gilbert's Bar House of Refuge. The house is perched on a thin outcrop of Anastasia rock between the ocean and the river. The "Bar" is actually short for sandbar, and "Gilbert" was a Colombian pirate, to whom you will be introduced to later in this book. Gilbert's Bar is the entire rocky reef that terminates at the Stuart Inlet and a very good reason why there were so many shipwrecks over the hundreds of years.

Gilbert's Bar House of Refuge was built on a craggy outcropping of Anastasia rock in 1875 as part of a system of coastal lifesaving houses. The U.S. Life-Saving Service, precursor of the Coast Guard, hired a lone "keeper" to man the house. He had to sign an oath of office and was saddled with the responsibility of maintenance of the house and servicing wrecked vessel survivors after storms. For this, he was paid the magnanimous sum of $400 annually. In 1915, the U.S. Life-Saving Service merged with the Revenue Cutter Service to form the United States Coast Guard. Gilbert's Bar House of Refuge became Coast Guard Station no. 207. It would retain this title until the end of World War II, when it was decommissioned. The property sat idle for eight years before being purchased by Martin County for the paltry sum of $168, with an agreement to spend $1,000 a year on maintaining it as a museum. It has been one of the premier historical sites in the area ever since. It is also one of my very favorite places on earth.

There have been countless shipwrecks on this coast due to a combination of jagged, shallow reefs and the ever-present threat of vicious storms. The Treasure Coast is in "hurricane alley," which means that it is in the common trajectory of the vicious storms that form off the coast of Africa every year. These storms often gain massive strength as they rage across the Atlantic, laying a path of devastation on hapless islands and coastal communities.

As I sit on one of the rockers on the porch at the House of Refuge, I try to imagine how forbidding the east coast of Florida was in the early days. Some of the shipwrecks were miles away from the House of Refuge. The keeper would have to find the wreck, rescue any survivors and then make the long journey back to the house. There was also the constant threat of opportunist wreckers who might get to the stricken vessels before he did.

Gazing out over the smooth, serene surface of the ocean, I remember how unforgiving it can be at times. I then wonder what it was like for travelers sailing up the Gulf Stream from Cuba on their way to Spain. They had no way of knowing if a hurricane was raging toward them. They could only rely on the intuition of the more experienced seamen on the ship to recognize the signs. Besides the threat of hurricanes, the most terrifying thing confronting these travelers was to be shipwrecked along the desolate, wild coast of La Florida. Legends of vicious cannibals who preyed on unfortunate shipwreck victims were common. The Spanish had maintained an uneasy alliance with the native coastal Indians known as the Ais for two centuries, and it was well known how brutal and fierce they were. Whether they were cannibals or not is up for debate, but some anthropologists agree that they may have practiced it not so much for sustenance but more for spiritual or religious

Many Spanish travelers heard the wild rumors of bloodthirsty "cannibals" that pounced on unlucky shipwreck survivors and were deathly afraid of suffering such a fate. The truth was that there was never any hard evidence found that Native Americans practiced this. *Florida Memory.*

reasons. Many native tribes of North America believed that to consume the flesh of their enemies was a way to absorb their power.

Another, and more plausible, fear that the maritime travelers experienced was the constant threat of pirate attacks on the high seas. Many of the ships carried tons of silver, gold, emeralds, pearls and other treasures from the New World. Tales of the Caribbean pirates were common, striking fear into passengers whenever another ship came into view. Many of the most prominent pirates of that age spent a good deal of time both near and on the shores of the Treasure Coast.

As you read these pages, it is our hope that you develop a deeper appreciation of the beautiful place we call home. Florida's Treasure Coast abounds with historical events that have had a lasting impression on the destiny of our entire country. Please join us as we explore the fascinating characters that make our home truly unique.

I

The Ancient Residents

In 1565, Pedro Menéndez de Avilés landed at the future site of St. Augustine, Florida, where he encountered the great Timucua people. Menéndez was there to remove a French colony of Huguenots who, two years prior, had settled about twenty miles to the north near the mouth of the St. Johns River at a place they named Fort Caroline. Already familiar with Europeans and their strange customs due to their previous interaction with the French, the Timucua were understandably suspicious of these newcomers. At first, relations with the Spanish were amiable, but things quickly degenerated as the natives realized that the newcomers were not leaving. The Timucua were a very powerful people but, in the long run, proved to be no match for Spanish guile, vicious brutality, powerful weapons and deadly European diseases.

To the south of their domain, starting near today's Daytona Beach, was an area designated as the "Land of Ais" on old Spanish maps. These Ais, or Ayz people, depending on which Spanish map from that period you use as a reference, proved to be a formidable foe of the Spanish for the next two hundred or so years. These were the original inhabitants of the area known today as the Treasure Coast. A strong and fiercely dominant people, the Ais resisted European conquest with great zeal. The Spanish never had enough manpower to properly police the entire east coast of La Florida or to dominate the numerous Ais, so the two sides maintained a reluctant alliance for many years. In addition to fish and game, they ate oysters, clams and snails from what is today called the Indian River. The

High Counselor. By artist Theodore Morris.

Spaniards referred to the river as the Rio d'Ays on all their maps. The Seminole people called it the Aysta-chatta-hatch-ee, or the "River of the Ais Indians."

The Ais were not what one would call an agricultural people, nor were they nomadic. Gatherers or foragers would be a more accurate description. The coastal settlements had such an abundant and stable food supply that they simply didn't have to work very hard to feed themselves. A wide assortment of fish and small whales, oysters, clams, small animals, birds and edible plant life were so plentiful that it only took a short time each day to sustain a very healthy diet.

How could the Ais Indians stand to live in the hot, mosquito-ridden environment of Southeast Florida? To answer this question, it is important to remember that most of our ancestors of European descent have only lived in Florida for a maximum of about five hundred years, with a huge surge in population since the advent of air conditioning. The Ais, Timucua and many other native tribes lived here for *thousands* of years. It boggles the mind to comprehend such time spans. These people were perfectly adapted to life in the South Florida environment. The weather patterns would have been like those of today. In the winter months, they would maintain their coastal settlements to fish and reap the benefits of the ocean on the barrier islands. When the summer months came, with waves of exhausting heat, hurricanes and hordes of insects, the Ais would retreat to their mainland settlements. They simply knew no other way of life. For this reason, they flourished and multiplied along the coast for many centuries. Whole cultures lived, laughed, cried, found lovers, had babies, worshipped their gods and died there. The Ais were so numerous that, when the Spanish arrived in the late sixteenth century, the newly appointed governor stated that he had never seen so many people. Many of their burial mounds and garbage middens (the ones that have not been destroyed by development) can still be found, if one knows where to look.

FLORIDA'S FIRST PIRATES

One of the activities that the Ais indulged in was piracy and kidnapping for ransom. At that time in history, the area of the Caribbean that ran from Cuba northward along the eastern Florida coast was known as the Bahama Channel. This route was heavily used by wind-borne shipping vessels for hundreds of years due to the natural three-knot currents of the Gulf Stream. The Bahama Channel was the most popular shipping lane of the time, especially for the great treasure galleons that made their way north laden with treasure that had been plundered from Mexico, South America and Asia. If they were traveling south, they would have been forced to avoid the natural northern current of the Gulf Stream by sailing inside the channel, even closer to shore. To avoid this, they had to sail on a long, roundabout journey that spanned thousands of miles. During the height of the Spanish conquest and plunder of South America, the hulking treasure galleons began their journey in Seville, Spain (later from Cadiz), and sailed down the coast of Africa to the Canary Islands, where they stopped for supplies. They then turned west to take advantage of the trade winds and, after sailing about a month or more, entered the Caribbean southeast of Puerto Rico. Here the convoy split into two: the Tierra Firme (Spanish name for the South American mainland) and the New Spain Fleets. After their holds were full of treasure and goods, they would rendezvous at Havana, Cuba, then the center of the Caribbean world. The ships would then leave in groups known as flotillas as a safeguard against piracy, taking advantage of the northern currents of the Gulf Stream to get back to Europe. This route took them along the coast of La Florida, near the wild, desolate coastal lands of the Ais, for hundreds of years.

The native people grew to resent the cruel, indifferent treatment of the Spanish invaders, so they gradually learned how to fight back. They quickly realized that the Spaniards had a great weakness for the chests full of gold and silver coins that filled the holds of the mighty galleons. The region has always been a magnet for hurricanes, so there were frequent shipwrecks along the coastline of their domain. When violent storms would rage across the Atlantic, unsuspecting vessels would often meet their end in the horrific winds and high seas. Despite the valiant efforts of the experienced seamen, these raging tropical cyclones would slowly push the wooden ships toward the shoreline, where the shallow, jagged reefs would tear their hulls to splinters. In the sixteenth century, the area now known as the Treasure Coast was a forbidding place to be shipwrecked. The low vegetation provided no cover from the brutal sun, and the voracious black clouds of mosquitoes and sand flies were maddening. Black bears posed a viable threat, especially during sea turtle nesting season, as they aggressively searched the beaches for the delicious eggs buried in the nests. Panthers were also prevalent, even on the barrier islands. Besides these dangers, the unfortunate soul who found himself stranded in this lonely, desolate paradise would face death by exposure, thirst or hunger.

The Ais and their subtribe to the south, the Jeaga, learned early on that prisoners taken from these shipwrecks could be exchanged for goods or Indian prisoners held captive by the Spanish. When a galleon wrecked on the reefs, the Ais would descend on the wreck in great screaming numbers, mercilessly slaughtering or enslaving the exhausted, terrified survivors and robbing the unfortunate vessel of any treasure. They would then carry whatever booty they had plundered back to their villages and bury it near the home of their leader, the Casseekey, for safekeeping. Captured survivors were often treated as currency, as they were shifted from village to village until the Casseekey could find the best deal for a trade. For these reasons, the Ais were known as the wealthiest tribe in the Americas at that time.

Pedro Menéndez de Avilés, 1565

After annihilating the French at Fort Caroline and establishing the fledgling colony of St. Augustine, Pedro Menéndez de Avilés took a tour of the Ais villages to the south. He had heard many tales of these fierce people and wanted to see them for himself. As he walked through one of these native settlements, he was shocked to see a white man among them. He was even more surprised when he heard the man's story. Eighteen years earlier, a Spanish merchant ship had wrecked on the coast near the village. The unfortunate survivors had been spilled out onto the hot sand with no water, food or any other necessities. The Ais warriors then attacked, brutally killing everyone except the one man. The reason they spared him was that he was a silversmith. The Ais warriors, vain about their appearance, treasured the earrings and pendants that the man could fashion. As the years passed, the white man gave up any hope of being rescued and eventually acclimated into the tribe, even taking a wife and having several mixed-race children. Even though the attack had occurred so many years' prior, Menéndez's

Pedro Menéndez de Avilés. *Public domain*.

temper brewed at the audacity of this violent attack on his countrymen. As he continued his tour of the Ais settlements, he secretly devised a plan for revenge. Back at the village where the Spaniard had been imprisoned, he announced that there would be a great celebration of unity. He and several of his soldiers entered the village, each taking a place next to an Ais warrior. At the height of the gathering, Menéndez stood and gave the prearranged signal, clapping his hands three times. Each one of his men then quickly pulled knives and swords, viciously stabbing the surprised, unsuspecting natives to death before they realized what was happening. Thus, began the gradual subjugation and cruel treatment of the indigenous tribes of South Florida.

TERRIFYING STORY, 1570

There was a story that swept through Caribbean ports that sent a chill of fear through any traveler who heard it. In 1570, a ship owned by a Spaniard named Alonso Centeno was transporting tons of animal hides from South America to Seville. His crew numbered thirty-five, with a few women and children onboard. As the vessel traveled up the Bahama Channel along the east coast of Florida, it was intercepted and captured by English pirates. The pirates took the passengers and crew to a barrier island known today as Jupiter Island, promising them that the local Jeaga Indians would not harm them due to an alliance with the Spanish. The native warriors greeted these unfortunate souls with open arms. What is interesting about this story is the relationship between the English pirates and the Jeaga Indians. Delivering their unfortunate Spanish captives to the natives would be a "win-win" for the pirates because they could conveniently get rid of any witnesses to their crimes. The Indians, on the other hand, placed a high value on captives, especially Spanish ones. They could trade their slaves with other tribes, like the Ais to the north or the mighty Calusa to the west. Prisoners were valuable bargaining chips.

For some unknown reason, the Jeaga chose a different path regarding these new prisoners. As soon as the pirates disappeared over the horizon, they fell on the Spanish captives with a vengeance, immediately hacking thirty men to pieces. The only lives that were spared were those of a young mother, her two daughters, her son and a sailor who was so badly wounded that he was near death. A short time later, Pedro Menéndez, nephew to the great conqueror Pedro Menéndez de Avilés, came to the area on a mission for his uncle. He was shocked to see the haggard surviving captives with the natives. Realizing that he did not have the manpower to overpower the mighty Jeaga, he offered to purchase these poor souls for the price of twenty ducats. The natives refused. Menéndez then used the Indians' own tactics against them. He traveled north to a nearby Ais settlement and captured six warriors. He then returned to the village and traded them for the prisoners.

JONATHAN DICKINSON, 1696

In 1696, the barkentine *Reformation* encountered bad weather off the coast of present-day Jupiter Island. Onboard was a Quaker by the name of Jonathan Dickinson who was en route from Jamaica to Philadelphia with his young wife and infant son. The vessel was shipwrecked on the island, all twenty-two souls left destitute on the wild coastline. They were discovered by two Jeaga warriors, whose frightening appearance and threatening gestures terrified the party. For whatever reason, the Indians chose to spare the bedraggled survivors, instead taking them prisoner. They then herded the Dickinson party approximately five miles south along the beach to a huge settlement on present day Jupiter Inlet:

> *About the eighth or ninth hour came two Indian men (being naked except a small piece of platted work of straws which just hid their private parts, and fastened behind with a horsetail in likeness made of a sort of silk grass) from the southward and running fiercely and foaming at the mouth having no weapons except their knives, and forthwith not making any stop; violently seized the first two of our men they met with who were carrying corn from the vessel to the top of the bank, where I stood to receive it and put it into a cask. They used no violence for the men resisted not but taking them under the arm brought them towards me. Their countenance was very furious and bloody. They had their hair tied up in a roll behind in which stuck two bones shaped one like a broad arrow, the other a spearhead. The rest of our men followed from the vessel, asking me what they should do whether they should get their guns and kill these two; but I persuaded them to be quiet, showing their inability to defend us from what would follow; but to put our trust in the Lord who was able to defend to the uttermost. I walked toward the place where our sick and lame were, the two Indian men following me. I told them the Indians were come and coming upon us. And while these two (letting the men loose) stood with a wild, furious countenance, looking upon us I bethought myself to give them some tobacco*

Above: "The Florida Indians Capture the Shipwrecked Company," from Pieter van der Aa, 1707. *Florida Memory Blog September 13, 2013.*

Left: Jonathan Dickinson's journal cover, 1720. *Public domain.*

G O D's
Protecting Providence,
M A N's
Sureſt HELP *and* DEFENCE,
IN
Times of Greateſt DIFFICULTY,
and moſt Eminent DANGER:
EVIDENCED
In the Remarkable Deliverance of ROBERT
BARROW, with divers other Perſons, from
the Devouring Waves of the SEA; amongſt
which they Suffered
S H I P W R A C K:
And alſo,
From the cruel Devouring Jaws of the Inhuman
Canibals of Florida.

Faithfully Related by one of the Perſons concern'd therein,
JONATHAN DICKENSON.

Pſal. xciii. 4. *The Lord on High is mightier than the Noiſe
of many Waters ; yea, than the mighty Waves of the Sea.*
—— lxxiv. 20. *The dark Places of the Earth are full of the
Habitations of Cruelty.*

The THIRD EDITION.

Printed in *Philadelphia*: Re-printed in *London*, and Sold
by the Aſſigns of *J. Sowle*, at the BIBLE in *George-
Yard, Lombard-Street,* 1 7 2 0.

and pipes, which they greedily snatched from me, and making a snuffling
noise like a wild beast, turned their backs upon us and run away.
—*Jonathan Dickinson,* God's Protecting Providence, *1699*

After a month, Dickinson and most of his party would eventually gain release from the Jeaga. The miserable party then began a torturous 230-mile trek north, slowly plodding along the beach all the way to the Spanish settlement of St. Augustine, Florida. They had very little clothing or supplies, so they were completely exposed to the elements. It was winter, so the farther north they traveled the colder it got. They also had to endure constant harassment by the Indians of several native settlements they passed for almost the entire journey. The journey was so harrowing and the hardships so great that several members of the party perished along the way. They were then rescued by the Spanish, who then sent them on to Charles Town (Charleston) in the colony of South Carolina. They later made it to Philadelphia, where Dickinson recovered and prospered. He went on to become mayor of Philadelphia twice, from 1712 to 1713 and again from 1717 to 1719. During those years, he wrote a detailed journal documenting his adventures in the wilds of Florida. Today, this short book contains the best description of the native people of the Treasure Coast that we have.

AIS TREASURE

There were thousands of shipwrecks along the Treasure Coast over a span of hundreds of years, many of them carrying vast amounts of treasure from places like Havana, Peru and Mexico City. The Ais wreckers were always there and became proficient at raiding these wrecks and absconding with any of the salvaged treasure. What they did with all of it is still up for conjecture today. It is well known that the Ais Casseekeys often had the loot secreted in great caches near their burial mounds in the forests of Southeast Florida for safekeeping. Sir John Hawkins (1532–1595) was an English slave trader who was among the first to profit from the "triangle trade" of goods and African slaves. John Sparks, chronicler of Hawkins's voyages, wrote about the riches of the Ais:

Gold and silver they want not, for the Frenchmen who first came here had
the same offered to them for little or nothing, and how they came of this gold

and silver the Frenchmen did not yet know, but by guess, and having traveled to the south of Cape Canaveral they found the same dangers by means of sundry banks, as we also have seen the same, and here finding masts which were the wrecks of Spaniards coming from Mexico.

Rene Laudonniere (1529–1574), a French Huguenot explorer confirmed that "the greatest part of these riches, washed, as they said, out of Spanish ships, which were commonly cast away in this strait."

In 1564, Jacques La Moyne, a French artist who sailed to Florida in 1563 with Jean Ribault, wrote this after gaining the written accounts of shipwreck survivors who had spent considerable time in the "Land of the Ays":

They also reported that this king possessed a great store of gold and silver, and that he kept in a certain village in a pit not less than a man's height in depth, and as large as a cask, and that if I could make my way to that place with a hundred arquebusiers, they could put all that wealth into my hands besides which I might obtain from the richer of the native. They said further, that, when women met for the purpose of dancing, they were, hanging at their girdles, flat plates of gold as large as quoits, and in such numbers that the weight fatigued and inconvenienced them in dancing, and that the men were similarly loaded. The greater part of this wealth, they were of the opinion, came from Spanish ships, of which numbers are wrecked in that strait, the rest from trade between the king and other chiefs in the neighborhood.

Hernando Fontaneda, a shipwreck survivor who lived among the Ais for several years, wrote about them in 1575:

The King of Ais and the Jeaga are poor Indians as regards the earth, for there are no lands of silver and gold where they are, and to say it at once, they are rich only by the sea from the many vessels which have been lost well laden with those metals….I desire to speak of the riches found by the Indians of Ais, which perhaps were to be as much as a million of dollars, or over, in bars of silver, in gold, and in jewelry made at the hands of Mexican Indians….

The country of the Kings of Ais and Jeaga is very poor. It contains neither gold or silver mines and to tell the truth it is only the sea which enriches it, since many vessels laden with precious metals are shipwrecked there.

Spanish coin found near an Indian settlement near Fort Pierce, Florida. *Author photo.*

Much of this treasure was never found. One problem is that much of Southeast Florida is now fully developed, with many of the suspected sites under blacktop or concrete. The true legacy of this native people may never truly be known. It could be buried right under our feet.

2

The Treasure Coast Is Born

On July 31, 1715, a tragic event occurred on the east coast of Florida that would prove to be so significant that it would not only send reverberations around the world but also mark the beginnings of a new age in the Caribbean. The most compelling thing about this event is the wild story behind it.

It was the year 1701, and the king of Spain was dying. Even though he was a member of the royal family, Charles II's life had not been a happy one. He was born deformed and possibly suffered from some form of mental retardation, most likely due to the heavy inbreeding prevalent in the royal families of that time. As a child, Charles had been unable to walk until four years of age and hadn't spoken a word until he was eight. Due his sickly nature and physical abnormalities, he was known in many circles as the "Bewitched One." He wandered around his home babbling incoherently, making outlandish requests of his staff. He had his ancestors dug up from their graves so he could sit and stare at them in wonder for days, perhaps contemplating his own unhappy existence. Despite this bizarre behavior, there was something about him that was even worse for a member of the royal family. Charles II was infertile.

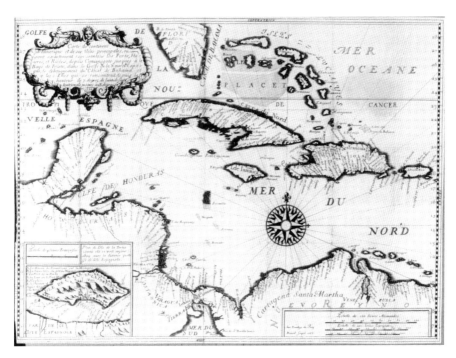

"Map of the Caribbean in French, 1686." *Engraving by Alexander Olivier Exquemelin, Library of Congress.*

Charles II of Spain.
Public domain.

TURMOIL IN EUROPE

Many of the leading royal families of Europe were related by blood, despite often being bitter enemies. Charles II was the last male member of the great House of Habsburg, whose members had ruled Spain since the sixteenth century. Now close to death with no heir, his passing signaled the end of the Spanish Habsburg line. The king of France, Louis XIV, was there at Charles's bedside.

It turns out that not only was Louis XIV married to Charles's half-sister, but he was also a member of the mighty Bourbon dynasty, with whom the Spanish Habsburgs had age-old alliances. Due to a complex lineage, the death of Charles II would mean that the Spanish crown would go to his sixteen-year-old grandnephew, Philip of Anjou, who was not only the king of France's grandson but also second in line to take over the throne of France after his older brother Louis, the duke of Burgundy. If young Philip accepted the Spanish crown, he would have to renounce his eligibility for the French one, but his ascendency would ensure a strong alliance between Spain and France. Louis XIV, ever the opportunist, was aware that this move would make his reign even stronger. The other powers of Europe vehemently protested this. England, the Dutch republic and another of Charles's distant relatives, Leopold I, emperor of the Holy Roman Empire, vehemently opposed what they saw as a Spanish-French monopoly. They all knew that this blood union would dramatically upset the delicate balance of power in Europe, and that war was inevitable. Thus began the bitter struggle for European dominance called the "War of Spanish Succession."

From the very inception of his reign, young Philip V's lands became embroiled in a vicious, prolonged war that he was—in a very real but indirect sense—responsible for. To make matters worse, he was born and raised in Anjou, France, so French was his main language. The new king of Spain did not speak a word of Spanish. One can easily imagine that these facts did not increase either his confidence or his effectiveness as a ruler.

Fast-forward to the year 1714. The War of Spanish Succession had finally ended—after thirteen long years. The mighty treasure empire that Spain had maintained in the Southern Hemisphere for over three hundred years was beginning to show cracks in its foundation. During the war years, the regular supply fleets could not sail from Havana to Spain safely because they were great targets for enemy ships. The treasure flow from the New World that had been steady for hundreds of years had practically ceased, but the

Felipe V de España, by Jean Ranc, 1723. *Public domain.*

heavy financial burden of war and the cost of maintaining the vast empire did not. For these reasons, the Spanish royalty was in dire financial straits.

Philip was so overwhelmed by pressure that he could barely rule. To make matters worse, his popular young wife, Maria Luisa of Savoy, suffered from

Elizabeth Farnese, Michel van Loo. *Public domain.*

"consumption," known today as tuberculosis. As was the custom of the day, physicians were not allowed to touch the queen with their hands, so they had to make their suggestions for her care from a distance. No doctor in his right mind would want to be the last to lay his hands on the beloved queen.

Maria soon perished. Her death sent Philip into such a tailspin of mourning and sadness that he had to be forcibly pulled from her bedside. He was frantic, depressed and possibly suicidal, so the worried Spanish chancellery came up with a plan: they would find their stricken king a new wife. They chose Elisabeth Farnese of Parma, Italy, an older woman. Legend has it that this fiery woman agreed to the union but refused to consummate it until an immense dowry arrived from Havana. A desperate, sex-deprived Philip sent word to all the admirals in South America and the Caribbean: Get the treasure fleets to Spain soon.

SPANISH CONQUEST

Spain had enjoyed free reign over Mexico and Central and South America for over three hundred years, ransacking their resources and exploiting their native populations. Throughout its newly "discovered" lands, the Spanish Crown forced the native populations to work in deplorable conditions in hellish silver and gold mines. During the colonial era, it is estimated that the notorious silver mine of Potosí in Bolivia alone produced up to forty-one thousand metric tons of silver. The silver and gold ore was then melted down and minted into roughly hewn coins. Examples of these are the "doubloon," a "32 real" (royal) coin and the "piece of eight," an "8 real" silver piece. To give a general idea of the coin's actual monetary value, one should note that the piece of eight was also known as the Spanish dollar. Not only were these coins used by the Spanish Crown to fund the high costs of maintaining its empire, but their hard value proved a worldwide currency as well. The colonists in early America traded with many of these same coins.

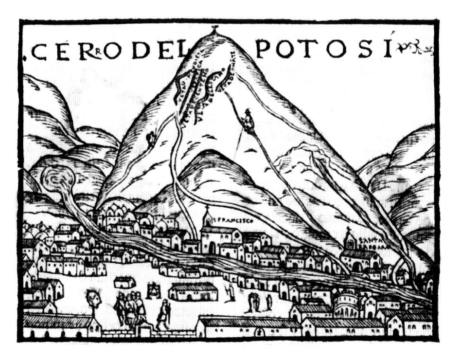

Potosí, the first image in Europe. Pedro Cieza de León, 1553. Public domain.

La Habana (Havana), Cuba, was the center of power and trade in the Caribbean at that time, and the place where all three main treasure fleets converged before the long trip back to Spain. These were the Tierra Firme Fleet, carrying treasure from Cartagena, Panama, Colombia and Peru; the New Spain Fleet, transporting gold and silver coins from mints in present-day Mexico; and the Manila Fleet, carrying vast treasures earlier transported across the Pacific Ocean from the Philippines and the Orient to Vera Cruz and painstakingly transported by muleback over the mountains to eastern ports. They would travel together back to Spain in great convoys known as flotillas as a safeguard against piracy. After leaving Cuba, they followed the same route they had used for centuries, taking advantage of the natural north-flowing currents of the Gulf Stream, slowly making their way past the area now known as the Treasure Coast. When the navigators caught sight of Cape Canaveral jutting out into the ocean before them, they turned west to cross the Atlantic to the Azores and then onward to Seville. With a combination of treacherous reefs and shoals and the constant threat of hurricanes, shipwrecks were not an uncommon occurrence on the desolate La Florida coast.

THE 1715 FLEET BEGINS THE JOURNEY

In La Habana, the admirals were experiencing great delays in getting the treasure fleets with their vast cargoes all together. They grew more nervous and agitated with each passing day. The fleet was long overdue, all the ships loaded to the water lines with gold, silver, emeralds, pearls and crates of porcelain china packed in thick mud. No manifest of the actual treasure was ever found, but it did include a seventy-four-carat emerald ring and fourteen-carat pearl earrings. The threat of piracy was so great that the admirals planned to travel as one great cohesive group up the coast, maintaining visibility between them. Hurricane season was fast approaching, and they knew that if they did not get underway soon, they may pay the price. After even more agonizing delays, they were finally ready to leave. There were twelve ships in all: six from the Tierra Firme Fleet, five from the Nueva España Fleet and one small French vessel, *El Grifon*, which came along for protection. Two war galleons were in the lead, with two more at the rear and an extra frigate carrying supplies. They were all charged with protecting the six treasure galleons loaded down with vast hordes of the king's treasure.

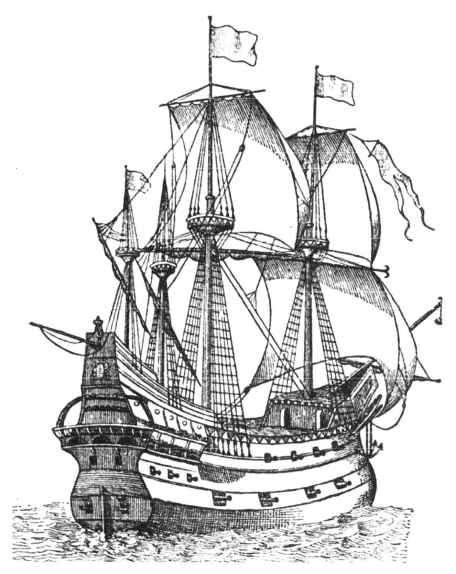

Spanish galleon. *Florida Memory*.

They left on June 24, 1715, a proud, magnificent treasure armada sailing slowly past El Morro Castle through the mouth of Havana Harbor. For five days, the weather conditions were ideal for a routine journey. Then, on July 30, the skies took an ominous turn. About midday, the wind suddenly died down to almost nothing; the heat and steamy wetness were nearly unbearable in the still air. The seas were calm, but there was a low, heavy swell coming in from the southeast that grew more pronounced as the day passed. As night fell, a thin haze began to move in, making visibility poor. The captain of the *Regla* signaled to light all the lanterns so that the ships might stay in sight of one another. One can imagine their soft glow in the distance, barely visible as they rose and fell through the milky vale of fog like ghostly spirits in the night. Tension seemed to grow among the crew as the old seamen and mariners started to mutter about aches and pains caused by impending inclement weather. There was an overall feeling of dread, and that night proved to be a long and sleepless one.

The next day proved no better, with the haze thicker yet and the swells growing higher and even more pronounced. The men on deck heard great sliding crashes from below as the weight of packing crates shifted, so they hurried below to secure them. The hatches were then closed and locked down and all sails shortened and reefed in preparation of the blow that they now knew was inevitable. Despite the early afternoon hour, the sky grew so dark that the lanterns had to be lit. The men did their best to push the ships to move faster, but it was difficult in the erratic wind. As soon as full night fell, the wind picked up to around forty knots, the sound of it shrieking through the rigging like the screams of a thousand banshees. To the sailors' horror, the ships began to pitch violently. The driving rains then began, drenching everything on deck and making visibility between the ships impossible in the darkness. The hapless crews valiantly tried to hold on and maintain their course, but the wind and rain worsened, making navigation impossible.

There was general panic onboard as the priests and friars started to wail out prayers that could barely be heard over the constant roar of the intensifying gale. The wind soon reached seventy-five knots, with the colossal waves increasing to twenty feet or better. Then, the worst of the sailors' fears were realized. The main mast splintered and bent to a bizarre angle, the rigging growing slack and becoming entangled into a great mess. All they could do was hold on for dear life and pray to Dios for safe deliverance. They watched in horror as giant waves surged over the railings, engulfing everything in their path, taking many sailors overboard with them. Despite all the efforts of the desperate crews, they found themselves immobilized, forced to watch as their great ships were slowly turned toward the shoreline by the howling, relentless wind and waves. They then had to stand by, completely helpless, as their wooden vessels were dashed and splintered on the sandbars and rocky shoals of the Florida coastline.

The next morning, the sun rose on utter destruction. The ships lay in ruins in the shallow waters of the beach for thirty miles, some on their sides with smashed hulls and masts bent at awkward angles, their tattered sails flapping gently in the calm, post-storm breeze. A few were standing upright but immoveable, and some were smashed into jagged heaps of floating boards and flotsam. Hundreds of battered and destitute survivors wandered dazedly along the shoreline, trying to find any sort of relief from the already blazing summer sun. Countless corpses bobbed gently in the surf; their peaceful slumber interrupted only by the sudden splash of the sharks as they feasted on the remains.

Those first days proved to be merciless on the survivors, with virtually no shelter, food or fresh water available. Some just dropped dead from the stress of the entire ordeal. At dusk, the sandflies would begin their merciless attacks, forcing many of the poor souls to bury themselves in sand up to their necks to escape the torturous assault. Small boats were sent north to the settlement of St. Augustine and south to Cuba. It took weeks for any rescue mission to be mounted.

Salvage

The wrecks were a financial disaster for the Spanish government. There were some reports that when he learned of it, King Philip V fell over into a dead faint. Not only did this devastate the Spanish economy, but it affected all the other countries that traded with Spain as well. Once the initial rescue effort was completed, the Spanish almost immediately set about salvaging the shipwrecks, establishing two crude camps near the present-day Sebastian Inlet. With incredible effort, the Spanish set about recovering everything they could. They recruited or enslaved the native Ais people who inhabited the area to dive down to the wrecks, as well as native pearl divers from the Caribbean islands. These men were forced to swim down to wrestle with the mire of planks and ropes and fumble through the chests and bring up what treasure they could find before losing their breath. Some would dive so deep that they would get the decompression illness known as the "bends" and either become crippled or die. If they did perish, there were plenty more slaves to spare. The Spanish utilized primitive diving bells that held pockets of air for the divers to use. Through their exhaustive efforts, they managed to recover over five million pieces of eight by the end of the year, an admirable sum when one considers the terrible conditions and lack of any sort of equipment. By the end of 1718, the Spanish authorities reported to Spain that nearly all the registered treasure had been recovered.

While a high percentage of the Spanish treasure was apparently reclaimed, it is important to note that rampant smuggling and falsified manifests were common on Spanish treasure ships. Everyone wanted their cut. It was very dangerous for the "plate fleets," as they were called, to make the journey from Cuba to Seville, and it seems that more treasure may have been unaccounted for than anyone realized. The Spanish royalty placed a high tax on everything brought to them. This was often set at 20 percent, also known as the "king's fifth." For this reason, smuggling aboard the treasure ships was very common. There were documented cases in which the ships were found to be carrying as much as twice the amount of silver shown on the actual manifest. For this reason, it has been widely accepted and often proven that huge amounts of treasure still lay scattered and buried in the shifting sands of the ocean's bottom along the Treasure Coast to this very day. Not only did the 1715 fleet disaster have a significant effect on the world's economy, but it would also signal the beginning of another era that would prove to be the wildest in the history of the Treasure Coast of Florida.

3

The Golden Age of Piracy

News of the 1715 fleet disaster soon traveled around the world, drawing buccaneers to the area like moths to a flame. Here was solid, irrefutable proof of how truly vulnerable Spain and its treasure galleons were. One of its most significant effects was that it attracted a different class of sailor to the Caribbean, much like sharks to a fresh kill. Nowhere was this more evident than on the island of New Providence, today's Nassau, where a lawless pirate kingdom was being established. The law-abiding residents of the island began to report run-ins with unsavory characters who had come there to find their fortunes. Navy ships reported of mass desertions, as their crews desperately tried to find a vessel that was headed for the Florida coast. Many of the infamous characters in the following section ended up in New Providence with a single goal in mind: to plunder Spain and its empire in the Americas.

The Allure of the Lifestyle

Piracy was nothing new to the Caribbean, but after the conclusion of the War of Spanish Succession, pirate attacks on the great treasure galleons increased with alarming frequency. This happened for many reasons, the most prominent being that, due to the dire need for cash flow in Spain, the number of transport voyages from Cuba increased.

Sketch by Don Maitz.

The slow-moving galleons were easy prey to an experienced captain with a quick sloop. Also, the war had ended, so there was a huge influx of thousands of unemployed sailors without any prospects. Back in London, sailors were looked at as the lowest form of man, so a life of struggling and poverty on the streets was not a favorable option. Most of these swarthy sailors had already spent large amounts of time in the warm waters and sandy beaches of the Caribbean and were familiar with the stories of the buccaneers. For years, they had regaled one another with tales of the exploits of swaggering outlaws like Henry Avery and Captain

Pirates used to do that to their captains now and then. *Artist Howard Pyle; public domain.*

Henry Morgan of Jamaica. Many of them now longed to follow in their footsteps and get rich by illicit means. Some of these young men would later become some of the most infamous pirates in history.

There were many reasons why an experienced sailing man would join a pirate crew. For one thing, pirate ships had none of the strict, brutal discipline of the navy. If they wanted to vote the captain out, they could do so by a majority vote.

Most pirate vessels divided prize loot into generous shares for the crew members. Some even had insurance deals in their articles. One of the most successful pirates of all time, Bartholomew Roberts, also known as "Black Bart," had a document of articles that all the crew members had to sign.

Articles
(1. Pirate captain's name) Captain Bartholomew Roberts
Drawn up by the (2. Pirate vessel's name) Good Fortune *crew as shipboard conduct*
I. Every man shall have an equal vote in affairs of moment. He shall have equal title to the fresh provisions, or strong liquors, at any time seized, and may use them at pleasure, unless a scarcity makes necessary, for the good of all, to vote a retrenchment.
II. Every man to be called fairly in turn, by list, on board of prizes because, they were on these occasions allowed a shift of clothes: but if they defrauded

the company to the value of a dollar in plate, jewels, or money, marooning was their punishment. If the robbery was only betwixt one another, they contented themselves with slitting the ears and nose of him that was guilty, and set him on shore, not in an uninhabited place, but somewhere, where he was sure to encounter hardships.

III. None shall game for money either with dice or cards.

IV. The lights and candles to be put out at eight o'clock at night: if any of the crew desire to drink after the hour they shall sit upon the open deck without lights.

V. To keep their peace, pistols, and cutlass clean and fit for service.

VI. No boy or woman to be allowed amongst them. If any man were to be found seducing any of the latter sex, and carried her to sea in disguise he shall suffer death.

VII. He that shall desert the ship or his quarters in time of battle shall be punished with death or marooning.

VIII. No striking one another on board, but every man's quarrels to be ended on shore, at sword and pistol.

IX. No man to talk of breaking up their way of living, till each had shared £1,000. If in order to this, any man should lose a limb, or become a cripple in their service, he was to have 800 dollars, out of the public stock, and for lesser hurts, proportionately.

X. The captain and quartermaster to receive two shares of prize: the master, boatswain, and gunner, one share and a half, and other officers one and a quarter.

XI. The musicians to have rest on the Sabbath Day, only by night, but the other six days and nights, not without special favour.

—*From Captain Charles Johnson's book,* A General History of the Pyrates, *first published in 1724*

CAPTAIN HENRY JENNINGS—PIRATE OR PRIVATEER?

The island of Jamaica was abuzz with the news of the fleet disaster, with every sailor in town making ready to sail for the Florida Coast to get his share. The frenzy was comparable to the California gold rush in 1849. They all were "goin' a wrecking." The craze went all the way up the ladder, with Royal Governor Archibald Hamilton even wanting in on the action. He asked several of his British navy associates to sail to Palmar De Ays and

Captain Henry Jennings. *Courtesy of the St. Augustine Pirate & Treasure Museum.*

salvage as much treasure as they could. After the proper, upstanding sailors refused to embark on what they considered to be a lowly mission, he turned to the many privateers, or professional maritime mercenaries, who lived on the island. Somewhat of a political zealot, Governor Hamilton already had several ships and captains prepared for war. He was planning to use his resources in New Providence in a planned rebellion to restore his beloved Stuarts to the English throne.

One of his privateers, Henry Jennings, was an experienced sailing captain who owned a good deal of land. Jennings took up the mission with gusto. His ship, the *Barsheba*, was one of those that was battle ready for missions in the service of Governor Hamilton. Upon acceptance of this new venture, he restocked his vessel with supplies, eighty sailors and many experienced native divers. The *Barsheba* then departed, making its way toward the Cuban coast. Jennings was accompanied by a well-known pirate named Charles Vane, who had a nasty reputation for violent behavior. A second vessel followed, Captain John Wills and his thirty-five-ton sloop *Eagle*, carrying as many as one hundred more hands. By December, they were approaching the South Florida coastline in search of evidence of the great disaster. When they arrived at Key Biscayne, they encountered another ship heading south. It was the *San Nicholas de Vari y San Joseph* carrying the mail from St. Augustine to Cuba. The captain, Pedro de la Vega, was "roughly questioned" by the pirates as to whether he had any knowledge of the location of the shipwrecks. It turned out that he had not only seen the wreck site firsthand, but he also had personally visited it. De la Vega also shared that his ship had already been plundered by English pirates who had already been "trying their hand" at salvaging one of the wrecks.

He told Captain Jennings and his men that if they wanted to find the wrecks all they had to do was let the natural current of the Gulf Stream carry them along the coast. Jennings then commandeered the *San Nicholas* as a prize and raised the Spanish colors as a ruse. The three ships calmly made their way north. The next day, they saw the remains of the first wreck, the *Nuestra Señora de las Nieves*. It lay on its side, the hull just above the waves, completely abandoned. The pirates then noticed a grim sight: several rough crosses planted in the sand to mark the final resting places of unfortunate victims. They soon passed more wrecks, including the *Urca de Lima*, a supply ship that had found refuge in the mouth of an inlet. As they moved northward, they came to realize that all the wrecks they encountered had already been picked over. Where had the Spanish taken all the treasure they had salvaged? Jennings, Vane and Wills hoped that their destiny lay farther north.

They passed what looked to be a small salvage camp. As Jennings observed it through his spyglass, he realized that it was quite small, with only a few huts, so he decided to keep looking. Six miles farther north, he found what he was looking for. His captive, de la Vega, told him that the place was called Palmar De Ays, named after the native people who lived in that area. Darkness had fallen, and all they could see was the distant glow of the campfires flickering softly in the cool sea breeze. Jennings divided his men into three groups. The heavily armed pirates quietly made their way to shore and prepared to attack. When the morning sun broke, the Spaniards inside the camp awoke to the sound of beating drums. The leader of the salvage effort, Admiral Francisco Salmon, had only sixty men with which to defend his buried loot. They scrambled around the camp in a panic, many of them abandoning their posts to flee into the surrounding woods. Admiral Salmon looked around at his pitiful force and weighed up his odds. Most of the treasure had already been moved to Havana, but they still possessed a large cache of silver. He summoned all his bravery and went out to confront the English invaders, meeting Jennings and his pirates on the beach.

"Is this war?" he asked.

The pirate's reply was terse and clear: "No, we came to fish the wrecks, to claim the mountain of wealth."

"There is nothing for you here. This treasure belongs to His Catholic Majesty, Philip V. We have been commissioned to secure it for him."

Admiral Salmon soon knew that his resistance was hopeless so, in a last desperate gamble, he offered the pirates 25,000 pieces of eight to leave. Jennings stubbornly refused, casually gesturing toward the rabble of bloodthirsty pirates. They broke and ran toward the makeshift camp, cutlasses in hand. Realizing that they were hopelessly outnumbered, the terrified, exhausted Spaniards quickly surrendered and disclosed the location of the buried loot. The pirates unearthed it and loaded it into their boats. They also took four bronze cannons and disabled three that were too large to move. They ended up with 350,000 pieces of eight, which they took back to Jamaica. While en route, they captured another Spanish ship for 60,000 more pieces of eight.

Jennings returned to the island triumphant and loaded with treasure. By that time, the treasure frenzy had grown to a fever pitch, increasing even more with the news of Jennings's success. Many navy vessels lost huge swaths of men to desertion. The raid on the Spanish salvage camp was technically an illegal act of war against the Spanish Crown, but Jennings had nothing to worry about from Governor Hamilton, who was very pleased with the results of the raid. The three captains had no problem at all with their new status. They were no longer privateers—they were hunted pirates.

After a short time, Henry Jennings and Charles Vane eventually decided to make another go of wrecking at Palmar De Ays, so the *Barsheba* and three other vessels were soon on their way back to the east coast of Florida. Along the coast of Cuba, they encountered an English vessel and decided to take it. It just so happened that pirates were already aboard, having earlier taken the ship. These men were led by a pair of young pirates, Samuel Bellamy and Paulsgrave Williams. Little did Jennings know that these two would soon gain much notoriety. When they saw Jennings's fleet of four ships approaching, Bellamy and Williams thought they were the authorities and panicked, frantically jumping into their small periagua to escape capture. The relieved English captain, whose name was Young, welcomed Jennings aboard, thinking that the *Barsheba* was a legitimate vessel rushing to his rescue. He soon regretted this move, as he discovered that his rescuers were also pirates.

Captain Jennings then formed a partnership with Bellamy, and together they attacked a French vessel, the *St. Marie*, plundering it. This alliance proved to be yet another decision that he would soon regret when Bellamy later double-crossed him. When the *Barsheba* eventually returned to Jamaica, Jennings's attack on the "neutral" French merchant ship created a political hornet's nest. He was now branded an out-and-out pirate by both the English and the French Crowns. He fled to New Providence Island, which by this time was a gathering place for the Brethren, as the pirates called themselves. Jennings was now safe and comfortable and set to living the life of a wealthy squire in a land of outlaws for the next two years.

In 1717, the king of England offered a pardon to all pirates who would swear off their illicit activities. The island of New Providence became divided into two factions: those who wanted to take the deal, and those who wanted to continue their pirating ways. Jennings chose to take the deal and moved back to Jamaica to surrender to authorities. He then became a pirate hunter, cruising the waters of the Caribbean in search of his old cronies. When the War of the Quadruple Alliance started, Jennings turned back to "legal" privateering, again experiencing a period of great prosperity.

There are conflicting stories about where Henry Jennings ended up. In one legend, he was captured by the Spanish and spent his last years rotting in a dank prison. Another story is that he retired a wealthy man in Jamaica and lived out his life as an honest, peaceful man. No one knows for sure. What we do know is that Henry Jennings was the original Treasure Coast pirate.

CHARLES VANE

One of the most notorious pirates in history, Charles Vane is believed to have begun his illicit career as a pirate around the year 1715 when he accompanied Henry Jennings on his trips to Palmar De Ays on the Florida Coast near present-day Sebastian, Florida. By that time, Vane had already

Charles Vane. *From* General History of the Pyrates, *1725.*

garnered a reputation for cruelty and general nastiness and was drawn to the freewheeling life of a buccaneer. For the next few years, he made New Providence in the Bahamas his home base as he cruised the Caribbean and surrounding waters for prizes. In the year 1718, the captains of two Bermuda-based vessels, the *Diamond* and the *William and Martha*, reported that Vane and his men had attacked their ships, brutally torturing and murdering several of the crew members. He was now a wanted man, on the short list of the great pirate hunter Woodes Rogers, who was at that time heading for the pirate haven of New Providence with the king's pardons.

Defiant to the end, Vane was the only pirate captain who blatantly refused the pardon deal. To escape the harbor that would soon be blocked by Rogers's three ships, Vane devised a bold and reckless plan. In the dark of night, he set fire to one of his prize ships and brazenly sailed it directly at Rogers's vessel *Rose*, causing it to burst into flames as well. In the ensuing confusion, Vane and his crew escaped with a hold full of stolen treasure. An enraged Woodes Rogers sent Benjamin Hornigold after the rebellious pirate. Hornigold was a notorious pirate captain who had signed the king's pardon and knew Vane well.

Vane then headed for South Carolina, where he preyed on ships doing commerce in and out of Charleston Harbor. It is believed that in 1718, he met up with his good friend Edward Teach (or Thatch), better known as Blackbeard, in a weeklong drunken orgy near Ocracoke Island. After this, he sailed back to attack ships near Charleston again, where he learned that the royal governor of Charleston had commissioned Colonel William Rhett and two armed sloops to hunt him down. The wily Vane then sent out a poorly hidden message that he intended to sail south. This news was soon intercepted by Rhett, who turned his ships in that direction in pursuit of the pirate. Vane had no intention of sailing south, turning north instead. Captain Charles Vane, through his cunning and prowess, had once more escaped capture.

In November of that same year, Vane and his crew were traveling through the Windward Passage when they encountered a vessel. Arrogant as always, Vane ran up the Jolly Roger and went after it. To his surprise, the ship was a heavily armed French man-o-war that turned its many guns on the pirates. Vane lost his nerve and made the decision to turn and flee. This choice proved to be quite unpopular with his rough crew, so the very next day they confronted him. They accused him of cowardice and decided to dispose of him and make Calico Jack Rackham the captain. An angry Vane and his closest men were placed into a small sloop and set adrift. Such was the life of a pirate.

Vane survived this ordeal but had to start again from scratch. He obtained another ship and slowly began to make his mark by attacking several vessels near the Bay of Honduras. In February 1719, his ship encountered a vicious storm and was heavily damaged. Most of his crew drowned, and he found himself marooned on a small island. Another ship happened to stop by and found him, but the news was not good. Captain Holford was an ex-pirate and knew Vane well. "Charles, I shan't trust you aboard my ship, unless I carry you a prisoner; for I shall have you caballing with my men, knock me on the head and run away with my ship a pirating."

Holford refused to take him on board, leaving a seething Vane to fend for himself. In an incredible stroke of luck, another ship came by. This time the crew did not recognize him and took him on board in an act of mercy. It seemed that Charles Vane's luck had finally changed. It had, but not for the better.

A few days later, the ship Vane was on saw another vessel approaching. As it drew closer, he was horrified to see that it was none other than his old friend Captain Holford's ship. Holford knew the captain and wanted to dine with him. When he came onboard, his blood ran cold as he instantly recognized Vane. He quickly informed the captain of the rescued sailor's identity. The captain then stated that he wanted nothing to do with the pirate, so he handed the unfortunate Vane over to Holford, who immediately hauled him onboard his ship as a prisoner in chains. Vane was then taken to Jamaica to face the music and be tried for the crime of piracy. Pirates were difficult to catch, but if one were, especially a pirate with the infamous reputation of Charles Vane, he had to be made an example of. On March 22, 1720, Charles Vane was found guilty of the crime of piracy on the high seas and hanged at Gallows Point. His body was then placed in an iron gibbet, or cage, and suspended in plain view at Gun Cay as a stark warning—*This is what happens to pirates.* It was a clear message that times were indeed changing and that the pirates' days of lawless unaccountability were numbered. The pirate Charles Vane will always be a significant part of the history of the Treasure Coast.

BLACK SAM BELLAMY

Samuel Bellamy. *Public domain.*

Sam Bellamy's story must be one of the greatest tales of accomplishment in history. Born around 1688, he had a tough upbringing in Devon, in the western part of England. He was the son of tenant farmers and most likely spent his youth in a nearly constant state of hunger. At some point, he ran away from home and ended up in one of the maritime port cities like Plymouth or Bristol. The War of Spanish Succession had just started, so he ended up on a seagoing vessel at the young age of thirteen, most likely the victim of one of the vicious press gangs that forcibly dragged men away to serve on a ship. English warships were drastically undermanned, so this practice was commonplace. Often the hapless victim of a press gang would never be seen again by his family or acquaintances. Young Sam was a ship's boy, forced to do all the menial onboard tasks. During the war years, Bellamy proved himself to be intelligent, resourceful and resilient. By the time the war ended thirteen years later, he had worked himself up to a master sailor, able to maintain and master the intricate workings of a ship. Like hundreds of other navy sailors, he suddenly found himself unemployed due to lack of any fighting. Like many, he had heard the legends of Henry Avery and Morgan and the riches they had found in the New World. Most historians agree that Bellamy sailed across the ocean to Boston and then to Cape Cod in search of his fortune around the year 1714.

There he made the acquaintance of a mild-mannered silversmith named Paulsgrave Williams from Rhode Island. The two men shared common interests and formed a fast friendship. Williams was from a wealthy family, which was just what Bellamy needed to help fulfill his dreams. Many people wonder why the thirty-eight-year old Williams would trade his calm, successful life for the unsure existence of a pirating treasure hunter. It may be that his father had been involved in shady businesses for his entire life, and Williams longed for more excitement.

MARY HALLET—THE SEA WITCH OF BILLINGSGATE

One of the most famous Bellamy legends is the tale of Mary Hallet. Around the year 1715, Bellamy was frequenting a bar somewhere in Eastham, near the cape. He met a sixteen-year-old girl named Mary Hallet. She listened in wonder to Samuel's tales of the sea and became smitten with him. The two fell in love and right away began a sexual relationship. Mary and Samuel were so serious that they went to Mary's parents to announce their impending marriage. Her father, a New England farmer, refused to let it happen. There was no way his daughter was going to marry, of all things, a penniless sailor with no prospects. Samuel reacted with anger, announcing that he was going to the Caribbean to make his fortune. He would then return to claim Mary as his own. Like hundreds of others, he and Paulsgrave Williams heard the news of the fleet disaster on the east coast of Florida. They made hasty preparations and left that same night, heading south toward the warm waters of the Caribbean. Much to her horror, young Mary soon realized that she was with child. This was completely unacceptable in the Puritanical society of the day, so Mary made the decision to conceal her condition. It is said that, several months later, she was discovered hiding in a barn with a dead infant in her arms. The town elders threw her in prison to stand trial for the murder. Mary lost her mind during her imprisonment and could be heard screaming uncontrollably though the night. She somehow escaped from the jail and made her way out to the flat lands, where she spent the rest of her days wandering aimlessly, terrifying the locals with her ghastly appearance. This is the legend of the Sea Witch of Billingsgate. Most historians are skeptical of the complete accuracy of this tale, but more than a few believe that there a few kernels of truth in this legend of the pirate and his young lover.

PALMAR DE AYS

When Captain Henry Jennings, John Wills and Charles Vane left the decimated camp at Palmar De Ays, the salvage operation was at full tilt. Now that the Spanish had been cleared out, the wreck sites were littered with several English vessels vying for the best position to dive and scoop up as many coins and jewels as they could from the shifting sands of the ocean bottom. Sam Bellamy and Paulsgrave Williams took their place among them, working long, brutal hours in the blistering Florida sun, diving alongside hundreds of other men. It turned out to be hellish work that was hardly worth the effort. The bulk of the treasure was still trapped in the holds of the ships, which were far from rotting away. They were unimpressed by the loot they collected, so their dreams of riches quickly turned to disillusion. When Spanish ships appeared on the horizon, they decided to make their way south.

They formed their own pirate band but were so poor that they were forced to operate out of a double-size ocean periagua. After they teamed up with Henry Jennings, their fortunes greatly improved. When they assisted the pirate captain in the successful attack on a French vessel, the *St. Marie*, Jennings was so impressed with Bellamy's sharp mind and practical tactics that they formed a temporary partnership. This was short-lived, however, as the young upstart double-crossed Jennings and took most of the treasure for himself. Bellamy and Paulsgrave Williams then partnered with the pirate Benjamin Hornigold. To Hornigold, all Spanish and French ships were fair game for attack, but ships from his native England were forbidden. One of Hornigold's officers was another well-known pirate named Edward Teach, or Blackbeard.

Samuel Bellamy, later known as "Black Sam," went on to become an incredibly successful pirate. When Benjamin Hornigold lost his ship to a mutiny that broke out over his refusal to attack English ships, Bellamy went out on his own, joining forces with the French pirate Olivier La Buse, better known as "Olivier the Vulture." They took many ships together, and Bellamy's reputation grew. He then took the greatest prize of all, the slave ship *Whydah*, a large vessel that would later hold twenty-eight cannons. Black Sam Bellamy and the *Whydah* soon garnered the most fearsome reputations in the Atlantic.

This excerpt is an account of a conversation with Black Sam from a "Captain Beer" after the pirate took his ship. Bellamy's words give a clear view of his mentality regarding his chosen profession:

I am sorry they won't let you have your sloop again, for I scorn to do any one a mischief, when it is not to my advantage; damn the sloop, we must sink her, and she might be of use to you. Though you are a sneaking puppy, and so are all those who will submit to be governed by laws which rich men have made for their own security; for the cowardly whelps have not the courage otherwise to defend what they get by knavery; but damn ye altogether: damn them for a pack of crafty rascals, and you, who serve them, for a parcel of hen-hearted numbskulls. They vilify us, the scoundrels do, when there is only this difference, they rob the poor under the cover of law, forsooth, and we plunder the rich under the protection of our own courage. Had you not better make then one of us, than sneak after these villains for employment?

In response to Bellamy's offer, Captain Beer told him that "his conscience would not allow him to break thro' the laws of God and man."

"You are a devilish conscientious rascal, damn ye," replied Bellamy "I am a free Prince, and I have as much Authority to make War on the whole World, as he who has a hundred Sail of Ships at Sea, and an Army of 100,000 Men in the Field…but there is no arguing with

Black Sam Bellamy's pirate flag. *Public domain.*

such sniveling Puppies, who allow Superiors to kick them about Deck at Pleasure; and pin their Faith upon a Pimp of a Parson; a Squab, who neither practices nor believes what he puts upon the chuckle-headed Fools he preaches to."

On April 26, 1717, the *Whydah* and three prize ships were caught in a vicious hurricane and wrecked on the rocks off the coast of New England. Out of 140 pirates to go into the churning water, only 2 survived. Black Sam Bellamy was not one of them. He never had the chance to gain the fame that he could have had—his pirate career was only one year long. In that short time, he had progressed from a penniless sailor without a ship to the most feared buccaneer in the Atlantic, commanding a fleet of vessels and over 200 pirates at the young age of twenty-one. This qualifies him as one of the most intriguing historical figures of all time. Black Sam Bellamy will forever be linked to the Treasure Coast of Florida.

THE MOST INFAMOUS EDWARD TEACH—BLACKBEARD

One of the most well-known pirates to show up in the Caribbean as a result of the Treasure Coast's 1715 fleet disaster was a man named Edward Teach—better known as "Blackbeard." He personally knew Black Sam Bellamy and Charles Vane and was one of the most feared and respected pirates of his time. Edward Teach (or Thatch) was born in the port city of Bristol, England, in the early 1680s. It is believed that he was an educated, resourceful man who, unlike most of the pirates of the time, could read and write fluently. He was intelligent and knowledgeable as a mariner and possessed great charisma in getting wild men to follow him. Tall, thin and intimidating, Blackbeard terrorized the Caribbean and Atlantic coast of the United States for several years.

In the year 1716, there were a great number of pirates gathering in Nassau. News of the 1715 wrecks had spread far and wide, and the influx of unemployed sailors and fortune hunters into the Caribbean was staggering. That is where the influential and powerful pirate captain Benjamin Hornigold gave a young Edward Teach, at that time one of his most devoted lieutenants, command of his first ship. Already an imposing figure, Teach insisted on wearing two braces of pistols and grew his beard out long. He then began to call himself "Blackbeard."

In the masterful work *The Republic of Pirates*, by Colin Woodard, there is a description of Blackbeard's frightful appearance by an early English historian:

> *This beard was black, which he suffered to grow an extravagant length. As to breadth, it came up to his eyes and like a frightful meteor, covered his whole face, and frightened America more than any comet that has appeared in a very long time. He would then tie the long strands into tight braids and tie a small ribbon on each one, giving him the appearance of a devil.*

He and another pirate, Stede Bonnet, became acquaintances and partners. Bonnet was a novice at sailing and piracy, but he was learned and wealthy—two things that Blackbeard admired. Known as the "Gentleman Pirate," Bonnet had switched to a life of piracy on a whim. When Blackbeard encountered him near the Bay of Honduras, he immediately took Bonnet's measure and decided to take advantage of the situation. Blackbeard imprisoned him on his own ship and placed his own crew in charge of sailing. When the two later parted ways, Bonnet was captured by the authorities and executed with several members of his unfortunate crew for the crime of piracy.

In 1717, Blackbeard took a large French slave ship, *La Concorde*, as a prize. The French crew later reported that Blackbeard had two ships; one with about 120 men and twelve cannons, and the other with around 30 men and eight cannons. The French surrendered after taking only two devastating volleys of fire. The cabin boy and 3 other French crew members joined Blackbeard's force willingly, and he forcibly took a pilot, 3 surgeons, 2 carpenters, 2 sailors and the cook. Blackbeard was obviously not interested in killing the remaining crew members or taking possession of the slaves that were held below decks, because he deposited them onshore on one of the nearby Grenadine Islands. What he was interested in was the French ship itself. Much larger than the one he was currently using, he commandeered the vessel and renamed it *Queen Anne's Revenge*.

Blackbeard spent the next several months cruising the Caribbean and taking many prizes. In early 1718, he headed north, arriving off the coast of South Carolina in May. In what could be considered the most daring and brazen act of his career, he blocked the port to Charleston completely, barring any ships from entering or leaving. Something must have gone terribly wrong onboard his four ships, because the only ransom he asked for was a large chest of medicine. After a whole week of blockading the harbor, the chest was delivered, and he turned his ships north.

Blackbeard. *Sketch by Don Maitz*.

A short time after the Charleston Harbor incident, two of Blackbeard's ships, the *Adventure* and the *Queen Anne's Revenge*, ran aground and had to be abandoned. Blackbeard's fleet attempted to enter Old Topsail Inlet in North Carolina, now known as Beaufort Inlet, and had apparently misjudged the depth of the water or the position of the reef. There is much speculation that Blackbeard did this intentionally because his crew had gotten so large that it might have been proving to be a liability. Blackbeard, not one to go down so easily, left on the third vessel with his handpicked crew and much of the best of the loot they had gathered in the preceding months.

Six months later, Blackbeard's ship and crew were lying dormant near Ocracoke Island near North Carolina. After a night of heavy debauchery, they were surprised in the early morning hours by the approach of two sloops commanded by Lieutenant Robert Maynard. One of the navy sloops ran aground, so Blackbeard's ship pounced on the opportunity by

Blackbeard the Pirate. *Public domain.*

pummeling it with a ripping broadside. Blackbeard's ship then made a run for the open sea, only to be slowed when a musket ball severed one of its main halyards and caused a mainsail to drop. The second navy sloop, with Maynard aboard, soon caught up with the fleeing pirates, but Blackbeard's guns sent another devastating broadside that killed over twenty of his men in an instant. Blackbeard, certain that the battle was over, pulled up alongside the still-smoking ship to board it. As soon as he set foot on the deck, dozens of Maynard's soldiers ran up from below decks where they had been hiding, screaming for revenge. A raging battle took place, and Blackbeard was killed along with several his men. According to Maynard, the pirate fell to the deck "with five shot in him, and 20 dismal cuts in several parts of his body."

Maynard returned to Virginia with a grotesque trophy for Governor Spotswood: Blackbeard's severed and withered head tied to his bowsprit. Blackbeard's reign of terror in the Atlantic had abruptly come to an end—or had it? There is a legend that, despite the grievous wounds administered to Blackbeard during the battle, his headless body swam around the ship several times. The fearsome reputation of William Teach, a.k.a. Blackbeard, lives on today. He will go down in history as the most notorious and well-known pirate of all time.

4

Don Pedro Gibert

A Wild, Untamed Land

In the early 1800s, the southeast coast of Florida was still a wild and untamed land. This was especially true on Hutchinson Island, a thin, barrier island that separates the mainland from the Atlantic Ocean near Stuart, Florida. In the early days, it would have been a wilderness coast with nothing but low, flat scrub as far as the eye could see, a seemingly deserted tropical paradise where one could encounter a black bear wandering out onto the beach to raid a sea turtle nest or hear the ominous scream of a panther. At times, especially in the winter months, it would have been a paradise in which dolphins played like children in the waves and great clouds of sea birds so numerous that they darkened the sky drifted gracefully along the coast in the relentless ocean breeze.

Incredibly remote and unsettled, the area known today as eastern Martin County was a decidedly hostile territory for most settlers from the north. The unrelenting heat, swarms of mosquitos and vicious storms added to the hardships of anyone who gave it a try. In 1803, a tenacious young man, James Hutchinson, obtained a land grant of two thousand acres on the Indian River from the Spanish governor of East Florida. His plans were to live there and build a prosperous plantation and farm. Fate was not with Hutchinson, because he soon realized that the local Seminole Indians were more than a mild nuisance. He complained that the they were molesting his

Bernardo de Soto. | **Don Pedro Gibert.**

Don Pedro Gibert and his first mate. *From the* Trial of the Twelve Spanish Pirates of the Schooner Panda, a Guinea Slaver, *Lemuel Gulliver, 1834.*

slaves, damaging his crops and stealing his cattle. Frustrated with the lack of available support, he forfeited his grant and had it transferred to a nearby barrier island he promptly named Hutchinson Island. He had decided to give his best efforts to a hardscrabble existence on this lonely strip of beautiful, but hostile, land. He soon began to have problems with "interlopers from the sea," whom he claimed were raiding his vegetable and fruit gardens. He went to St. Augustine to have a private conference with the governor and make a formal protest about the "pirates" who "burned his buildings, stole his slaves, and ruined his crops." He then embarked on the journey back home. Unfortunately for James Hutchinson, the boat he was on encountered trouble at sea and he drowned in a terrible accident.

The reef just north of where the present-day Stuart Inlet lies is called Gilbert's Bar (short for sandbar). It is widely believed that its namesake,

Don Pedro Gibert (the name was corrupted over the years to Gilbert), called the area his sometime home. Legend has it that this notorious pirate and his crew chose to pass their days on the high, natural sand banks, lying in wait for unsuspecting vessels that ventured in close to the shoreline on their journey north along the Gulf Stream.

SON OF THE SEA

Pedro Gibert was born in Catalonia, Spain, around the year 1800. He grew to love the sea from a very early age and quickly rose to the rank of captain on a merchant vessel. His country was involved in a great surge of trade with the Americas, so he decided to sail to the Caribbean to make his fortune. After proving himself a capable sailing captain, he obtained letters of marque from his government, becoming a privateer with permission to raid enemy ships. A handsome, reckless and impatient man, he decided that he was more suited for a life of piracy and smuggling. He became involved in the smuggling of cigars, liquor and tobacco. He also started robbing and plundering ships from various hiding places along the Atlantic coastline. It is said that he particularly liked the area around the present-day Stuart Inlet because there were countless creeks and tributaries where he could hide his sloop, the *Panda*.

When a possible prize was spotted by his lookout, he would use a variety of tactics to attack it. He would have his men light fires on the ocean beach to make it look as though they were shipwrecked and then try to lure the unsuspecting ship onto the rocky reef to meet its imminent destruction. This method, known as "wrecking," was very popular at the time. Gilbert's Bar has a large amount of exposed shell rock formations, known as Anastasia rock, along its coastline, making it an excellent place for this method of pillage. Today, in the place now known as Jensen Beach, there are a series of natural hills, part of the Atlantic Ridge of eastern Florida, that run close to the coastline. The legend states that Gibert used the sand-covered peaks, then known by mariners as "Bleech Yards," as a lookout place for ships sailing up the coastline. One peak, known by many as "Mount Pisgah," was one of the highest in the area, towering above all at fifty-seven feet above sea level. According to legend, this was the spot the pirate chose to use as a vantage point. When his lookout signaled to him that a vessel was approaching, Gibert's low-draft sloop would scoot out over one of the many fickle, sandy inlets in pursuit.

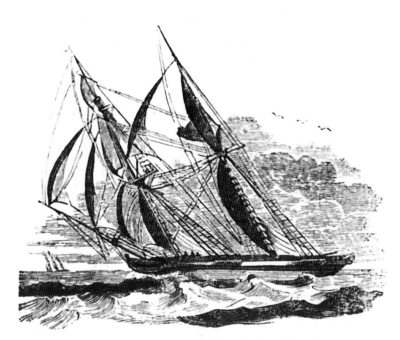

The Panda standing through the Bahama Channel.

The *Panda*. *From the* Trial of the Twelve Spanish Pirates of the Schooner Panda, a Guinea Slaver, *Lemuel Gulliver, 1834.*

DEAD CATS DON'T MEW—YOU KNOW WHAT TO DO

Don Pedro Gibert may have not been the cruelest and most bloodthirsty of pirates, but he certainly would have held a high position in their ranks. His gang of thugs would board the captured or wrecked vessel and immediately commence to beating the crew members mercilessly until they divulged where the real valuables were hidden. He would then dispatch all witnesses before destroying the ship. He practiced no quarter, believing that it was not in his best interests to leave survivors.

On September 20, 1832, the brigantine *Mexican* was sailing from Salem, Massachusetts, to Rio de Janeiro with ten boxes of money containing a total of $20,000. At 4:00 a.m., the watch noticed a vessel approaching from the rear. After stashing the money boxes in a hiding place, Captain Butman sent

The Mate begging his Life.

The mate begs for his life. *From the* Trial of the Twelve Spanish Pirates of the Schooner Panda, a Guinea Slaver, *Lemuel Gulliver, 1834.*

a small welcome craft over to greet the ship and was shocked to see the deck thick with pirates. They were soon back on the deck of the *Mexican* with several of the bloodthirsty invaders who proceeded to brutalize the captain and several of the crew members for hours, demanding that they disclose the location of the money. Eventually, they learned where the treasure was and set about the next phase of their dastardly plan. Don Pedro Gibert then issued his deadly decree: "Dead cats don't mew—you know what to do."

The pirates then did a truly terrible thing. They tied the *Mexican*'s crew members' arms and legs and placed them in the ship's hold, which they then shut tightly and secured. The rigging ropes were then severed, the sails slashed, and the ship set on fire.

The pirate gang then sailed off, leaving the *Mexican* and its crew to their fate. Fortunately, some of the men were able to get free and save the ship. Captain Butman put the fires out and limped his vessel back to Salem.

FUGITIVES FROM THE LAW

Gibert and his pirate crew were now hunted men. The American and British naval forces had formed an alliance to stamp out piracy, so they were both scouring the seas for illicit activity. In 1834, a British vessel, the HMS *Curlew*, spotted a ship that fit the description of the *Panda* off the coast of West Africa near the Nazareth River. The captain, Henry Dundas Trotter, had recently learned of the search for Don Pedro Gibert and decided to investigate. When the *Curlew* got close, the crew saw that the pirates were fleeing the *Panda* in small boats. They gave chase but soon gave up and returned to the pirate schooner. There they found that one of the pirates had lit a fuse to a hidden powder keg as a booby trap.

The Pirates carrying Rum on Shore to purchase Slaves.

Pirate carrying rum. *From the* Trial of the Twelve Spanish Pirates of the Schooner Panda, a Guinea Slaver, *Lemuel Gulliver, 1834.*

After extinguishing the fuse, they took command of the *Panda* and sailed it up the river in pursuit. Twelve days later, as they approached a place called Cape Lopez, the *Panda* suddenly exploded. The true cause of the blast was never discovered, but there was most likely some forgotten gunpowder deep in the hold that somehow ignited. Out of the twenty-five men aboard, two officers and two sailors were killed in the explosion. Captain Trotter himself was thrown into the sea by the force of the explosion, narrowly escaping injury. Enraged, he continued his search on land, eventually capturing Gibert and several of his men.

The prisoners were taken back to Salem, Massachusetts, then transferred to Boston, where they would be tried. The Golden Age of Piracy had ended one hundred years earlier. It was 1834, and everyone was curious.

THE SENSATIONAL TRIAL

The fourteen-day trial was indeed a circus, with emotions running so high in the courtroom that actual blows were thrown. In the end, Don Pedro Gibert and six crew members were found guilty of the crime of piracy. Only four of them were sentenced to hang because Gibert's first mate, Bernardo De Soto, had assisted with the rescue of dozens of Americans from a burning boat in the Bahamas four years earlier. Another convicted pirate, Ruiz, was shown leniency because of his "insanity." Five more of the pirates were acquitted for various reasons. Gibert steadfastly maintained his innocence through the whole affair, despite the overwhelming evidence against him.

In those times, there were no televisions, radio or broadcast sporting events, so a trial of this magnitude incited a lot of excitement in the general populace. This event generated even more news because it was a *pirate* trial. Many were elated that there would be hangings. People would often struggle through crowds to get close enough to get a good view of this grisly form of execution. In those days, hangings were often theatrical events, with the condemned required to make a last statement to the crowd before the noose was slipped over his head.

The evidence against the Spanish pirates was indeed damning. One of the most riveting accounts of the attack was provided by the Captain John Groves Butman of the *Mexican*:

TRIAL OF THE TWELVE
SPANISH PIRATES

OF THE

Schooner PANDA, a Guinea Slaver,

CONSISTING OF

DON PEDRO GIBERT, Captain; *Bernardo de Soto*, Mate; *Francisco Ruiz*, Carpenter; *Antonio Ferrer, the tattooed Cook*; *Nicola Costa*, *Manuel Boyga*, *Domingo de Guzman*, *Juan Antonio Portana*, *Manuel Castillo*, *Angel Garcia*, *Jose Velazquez*, and *Juan Montenegro*, Seamen,

For Robbery and Piracy, committed on board the Brig Mexican, 20th Sept. 1832.

The Black King, at Cape Lopez, who protected the Crew of the Panda.

BOSTON:
PUBLISHED BY LEMUEL GULLIVER, 82, STATE STREET.

1834.

A Pirate's Long Knife.

Trial advertisement. *From the* Trial of the Twelve Spanish Pirates of the Schooner Panda, a Guinea Slaver, *Lemuel Gulliver, 1834.*

When we got onboard the brig, they directed me to go into the cabin, which I did, and two or three of them followed. When I reached the cabin, two or three of them presented their knives to my breast, and demanded the money that was on board the vessel—I was alarmed and told them where it was. The money was in the run, under the cabin—called my mate come and get the money—he came down, and some of the crew with him. The pirates then told them to get the money up immediately—beating them with the handles of their knives, because they did not work fast enough. The boxes containing the money were marked P, and were handed on deck as they were got up from the run. The knives used by the pirates were large, and about three inches from the point were double-edged. The men in the cabin said I had more money, and went searching about, overhauling our chests and berths—one of them said if they found more money, they would cut my throat immediately. They went to another part of the vessel and left me alone. In a few minutes I attempted to go off deck to see what was doing, and one of them drove me back, and insisted I had more money. A short time later another came down, and insisted I had more money. He had my speaking trumpet in his hand and beat me with it severely.

A short time after, I saw the boat going toward the schooner, with the boxes—saw them out the cabin window—the boat was their own. In about fifteen minutes, saw a boat full of them coming back again—think there were about twelve in all—heard them jump on deck, close the cabin doors and after—hatchway—heard a great noise, as if the yards were coming down—could hear the main boom flying from side to side. The crew by this time were below, most of them in the cabin—forecastle hatch was fastened. Heard them heave a spar off, which I had lashed to the davits—smelled smoke shortly afterwards. I then saw them, from the cabin window, go to their vessel—they had my boats and one of my spars with them. They hoisted in their own boat, and I suppose they scuttled mine, as she filled with water immediately after they casted her off. The schooner then made sail from the brig. When they were at a sufficient distance, I got up out of the cabin skylight, which they had neglected to fasten—found everything in disorder, the rigging, yards, all flying about—all the running rigging and halyards were cut away. The sails were also cut to pieces—the main sail was hanging over the caboose, the roof of which was on fire—found a tub of tarred rope chains in the caboose—If we had not come upon deck at that moment, the caboose would have set the mainsail on fire, and then nothing could have saved the vessel. The mainsail was cut into strips—could not swear that any of the

men present were those who boarded the Mexican—*saw and recognized
a man who landed with these prisoners—saw him at the Town Hall—at
Salem. The man to whom I allude recently committed suicide in jail. He
was one of the two who drew their knives on me in the cabin.*

The Sabin American Print Edition, Report of the Trial of Pedro
Gilbert. *Boston: Russell, Odiorne & Metcalf. From Providence:
Marshall Brown and Co.; Portland: Colman & Chisolm; Salem: John
M. Ives, 1834.*

The day before Gibert's execution, one of the condemned men tried to
slit his own throat with a piece of tin. He was unsuccessful in his suicide
attempt, but he did manage to lose a lot of blood. He was so weak at the
hanging that he had to sit in a chair on the gallows stage. On June 11, 1835,
Don Pedro Gibert, Boyga, Castillo, Garcia and Montenegro met their maker
on the gallows at the Leverett Street Jail in Boston, Massachusetts, in front
of twenty-thousand people. Don Pedro Gibert's illustrious career as a pirate
and smuggler had come to a violent end. Today, Gibert's memory remains
alive as one of the most well-known pirates of the Treasure Coast.

5

Smuggling and the Slave Trade

The tradition of smuggling and the slave trade in the region known today as Florida's Treasure Coast did not originate with the arrival of Europeans. The area's original inhabitants practiced it long before any white men ever set foot on its shores. For thousands of years, people have benefited from the southeastern coast's proximity to the Bahamas and the main shipping routes from South America. There were several distinctive groups of native people who resided there for long periods of time, the most recent and well known being the Seminole. In order to explore the history of smuggling and the slave trade on the east coast of Florida, one must have a basic knowledge of the politics and military struggles of the time. The Seminole Wars of the early and mid-nineteenth century endured for nearly forty years and left a permanent impression on the history of Florida's Treasure Coast.

LATECOMERS TO FLORIDA

When most people think of Florida Indians, the name Seminole comes to mind. In order to appreciate the history of the area, the origins of this tough and resilient people must be considered. Even though the Seminole Indians thrived in Florida for hundreds of years, they were not the original

Marines battle Seminole Indians in the Florida War, 1835–42. *Public domain.*

inhabitants. They didn't start coming into Florida en masse until the late 1600s. They were, for the most part, descended from the Creek people of South Carolina and Georgia and were driven into northern Florida by the white landowners to the north. Seminole is a corruption of the Creek word *simanó-li*, which means "outcast" or "runaway." This term may also have been derived from the Spanish word *cimarrones*, which means "wild ones," or "those who broke away."

After the War of 1812 ended, Andrew Jackson, the "Hero of New Orleans," took it upon himself to settle all his old scores. He had always maintained a strong resentment against two factions with equal intensity: the British and the Native Americans. Under his command, the U.S. Army declared war on the Red Stick Creek Indians, who were raiding white settlements in retaliation of white encroachment on their lands. In 1814, he won a great victory over them at the Battle of Horseshoe Bend in the Mississippi Territory, thus bringing an end to the Creek War. Many of the native survivors of this struggle fled south across the border into Spanish Florida.

At that time in history, the idea of Manifest Destiny was very strong. America was growing by leaps and bounds, and the idea of a vast empire stretching "from sea to shining sea" was rampant. From Andrew Jackson's point of view, the unexplored swampland of Florida was a constant thorn in the side of the new nation. Still in Spanish hands, it was a source of endless complaints from Georgia and South Carolina plantation owners. They stated that their slaves were escaping and slipping across the border into Florida to find refuge with the Seminole Indians who lived there. They wanted their property returned to them. On April 8, 1816, General Andrew Jackson, then in charge of the Southern Military District, ordered General Edmund P. Gaines to take his forces into Florida to attack a fort named Prospect Bluff that overlooked the Apalachicola River. At the time, the "Negro fort" stronghold was

President Andrew Jackson, "Sharp Knife" to the Seminoles. *Library of Congress.*

full of over 300 rebellious and heavily armed runaway slaves, along with several women and children. During the engagement, an errant shot from a U.S. Army cannon hit a full powder magazine, causing a massive explosion that destroyed the fort and instantly killed 270 of those trapped inside. The survivors were taken prisoner and either sold as slaves or tortured to death by the soldiers. This event only succeeded in exacerbating relations with the tough Seminole Indians, who increased their raids on white settlements along the border in retaliation.

THE FIRST SEMINOLE WAR, 1817–18

Tensions with the Seminoles came to a boiling point on November 21, 1817, when Gaines ordered Major David Twiggs to attack a contingent of Seminoles at a place called Fowltown near the border. On November 30, 1817, a supply party boat was attacked by angry Seminole warriors on the Apalachicola River, resulting in the Scott Massacre, in which several soldiers, women and children were supposedly slaughtered by vengeful Seminole warriors. Andrew Jackson smoldered at this, as well as the thought of Florida as a vast Indian and escaped slave sanctuary, so he decided to act.

In 1818, he created an international incident by leading U.S. forces into northern Spanish Florida. When he arrived at the destroyed Prospect Bluff, he ordered a new structure to be erected, renaming it Fort Gadsden. He then illegally attacked the Spanish fort at St. Marks, where he hanged two Seminole leaders and ordered the execution of two British agents whom he suspected of treason. He then moved on to take the Spanish Fort San Carlos de Barrancas at Pensacola before declaring victory. This short, but violent, encounter would forever be known as the First Seminole War, an incursion that did very little to subdue the rebellious Seminole people.

One positive result for the United States was that Jackson's military "victories" led to the 1819 Transcontinental Treaty with Spain, which ceded Florida to the United States. The relentless push of the white plantation owners started in force to claim the bountiful ranch lands of northern Florida. This meant that the Seminole Indians would now have to fight or move farther south.

The Second Seminole War, 1835–42

As the years passed, the whites pushed deeper into the Florida territory, relentlessly encroaching on native lands. In 1832, the U.S. government presented the Seminoles with yet another document designed to completely remove them from Florida. The Treaty of Payne's Landing gave the Seminoles three years to relocate to Oklahoma Territory. One of the Seminole Indians, a young, flamboyant warrior named Osceola, was particularly vocal about his disdain for the whites and their covetous ways. He could never be a true chief due to the mixed-blood of a Scottish trader and a Seminole mother that ran through his veins, but the young firebrand held great influence over the tribe and was their most powerful asset during the war. He wanted nothing to do with the U.S. government and stubbornly refused to believe anything the "Great Father" said.

On December 28, 1835, the tensions between the Seminoles once again erupted into violence. On the trail from Fort Brooke (Tampa) to Fort King near present-day Bushnell, Florida, an army of vengeful Seminole warriors surprised a contingent of 110 soldiers under Colonel Francis Dade. The Indians slaughtered them all except for 3 terrified men who feigned death, lying motionless for hours until the Indians left. This violent incident would forever be known as the Dade Massacre. At the same time,

"I will make the white man red with blood; and then blacken him in the sun and rain...and the buzzards live upon his flesh"—Osceola, 1832. *Library of Congress*.

Osceola and his men rose in furious, calculated defiance and killed 6 men at Fort King, including an Indian agent named Wiley Thompson. The warriors then scalped the bodies, displaying the grisly trophies in a raucous, howling victory celebration back at their village. This was the beginning of the Second Seminole War, a bloody conflict that would go on for seven long years. This struggle would prove to be one of the costliest wars in

U.S. history and would end indecisively, with the Seminoles retreating to their Everglades strongholds and the soldiers to their forts. Due to the logistical difficulties of fighting an elusive, cunning enemy in the worst of conditions, the Second Seminole War damaged the reputation of every officer who participated in it.

The Third Seminole War, 1855–58

In 1855, the leader of a prominent Seminole family named Billy Bowlegs was living a quiet existence on Seminole land in South Florida. A group of U.S. Army engineers and surveyors ventured onto this land with orders to scope out Indian holdings in the area. Even though they were supposedly under orders to do nothing to anger the Seminoles, they took it upon themselves to destroy many of the crops and fruit trees there. Many historians believe that this was an intentional provocation by the army to justify a military response. When Chief Bowlegs saw what had been done to his land, he angrily retaliated by organizing forty of his warriors and resumed violent raids on nearby white settlements. This began the struggle known as the Third Seminole War. After three years of lopsided skirmishes, Bowlegs's numbers were severely diminished. In 1858, the U.S. government offered Billy Bowlegs $7,500 to relocate to the Oklahoma Territory. Each of his chiefs would get $1,000, warriors $500 and each woman and child $100. They were paid as they boarded the ship on Egmont Key in Tampa Bay that would take them to Fort Pike in Louisiana and then on to a reservation in Oklahoma.

There were only about two hundred Seminole Indians left deep in the Everglades. There were two factions present. The leader of the Muskogee people was named Chipco, and the Mikasuki were led by a cunning wise man named Abiaca, or Arpeika. The soldiers couldn't pronounce his name, so they called him "Sam Jones." He stubbornly refused to deal with or listen to anything the whites said. Sam Jones would go on to become the spiritual leader of his people for many years afterward. These two to three hundred remaining people were the direct genealogical ancestors of the Seminole and Mikasuki people today.

The Seminole Wars lasted for nearly forty years, resulting in the expenditure of hundreds of lives on both sides and costing tens of millions of dollars. This was all to no avail, because a treaty was never signed. The Seminoles, to this day, remain the only unconquered Indian tribe in America. One of the reasons the U.S. Army failed was the harsh and extreme conditions of the Florida Everglades. As the fighting slowly moved southward down the peninsula, the soldiers found that they simply could not fight in the swamps during the summer months. Their gun powder was wet and useless, some had no shoes and many were sick with the mosquito-borne illness malaria. They called this "the sickly season" and quit fighting completely for months until the oppressive conditions of southern Florida lifted. Also, the Seminoles were excellent fighters, utilizing guerrilla tactics in the swamp against the poorly supplied, unsuspecting soldiers. They were, after all, in their own home and understood the terrain far better than the generals. When the battles started to tilt in favor of the more numerous soldiers, the Seminole warriors would simply melt back into the trees like spirits, escaping to fight another day.

Outside Aid for the Seminoles

There is an abundance of evidence that all through the war years, the Seminole Indians were aided by the Spanish and British smugglers and even by some American whites. There also is a high probability that much of this activity was even sanctioned by the Spanish and English governments. At every single engagement, the Seminoles seemed to have better weapons than the U.S. Army. How could this be? It became obvious to the army that someone was supplying the natives with arms, powder and shot and basic supplies. The tough, resilient Seminole warriors were a consistently powerful nemesis to the U.S. Army due to smuggled assistance from outside forces.

One of the most convenient places to supply the Seminole warriors were the inlets and creeks located along the area known today as the Treasure Coast. When the goods arrived, the Seminoles would pay the smugglers with jerked and salted beef from their extensive cattle holdings. Many U.S. military officials suspected the Cuban government of this subterfuge, but it was never proven. The Spanish were deeply resentful of the U.S. government due to the disputed Florida territory, so it is highly likely that they smuggled weapons, powder, shot, salt and other goods to the Seminole fighters throughout the war years. Whether this supply chain was implemented through Spanish fishermen, the masters of Spanish trading vessels, or Spanish nationals from Cuba is uncertain, but the frequent reports of large military vessels with mounted guns at different places like Key West and the Tampa coast are very telling. Some of the strongest evidence of Spanish aid was provided by captured prisoners.

ENCOUNTER AT JUPITER, FLORIDA

Before the first Battle of the Loxahatchee in January 1838, Lieutenant Levin Powell of the U.S. Navy's Waterborne Everglades Expeditionary Unit was scouting the river for Seminole encampments near present-day Jupiter, Florida. His party of sailors came upon a mixed-race man on the river with a boat full of powder and shot. Powell's men detained and questioned him, and he eventually admitted that he was a runner for the Seminoles. He also shared that he had procured the goods in Havana, Cuba. When Powell and his men ventured into the forest to find the Seminole camp, they were surprised by a contingent of tough Seminole warriors and soundly defeated. The Seminole warriors had better weapons and plenty of ammunition and were well hidden in the palmetto scrub.

There were numerous incidents of Spanish smuggling on Florida's west coast as well. As for the later marijuana smugglers of the 1960s, the intricate maze of islands, creeks and tributaries provided a good place for weapons smugglers to operate their trade.

In December 1842, a local resident claimed that he had witnessed the following:

> *"seven or eight vessels at a time inside the bar at the inlet, and that it was even now visited by the wreckers, and offers them a place of resort and deposite* [sic]*, from which merchandise, sugar, tobacco, and segars* [cigars] *in particular, could be shipped to any ports of the United States, as Florida produce." This citizen wished to emphasize the attention of the Secretary "the facilities afforded to the smuggling of contraband articles, and particularly Cigars of Spanish Manufacture, and Indian River Inlet and Gilberts Bar, from their contiguity to the West India Islands."*
> —*Toni Carrier, University of South Florida, 2005*

The same man also reported that he possessed knowledge that two other inlets, the ones at both Gilbert's Bar and Jupiter, were often used by the wreckers at high tide, when they were deep enough to accommodate low-draft vessels. One year later, another Fort Pierce resident reported to the secretary of the treasury that the schooner *Ellen* entered the bar at Indian River and illegally landed a cargo of salt. According to this account, when a Coast Guard cutter came into view, a ship's manifest was hastily drawn up that did not include the salt that had been landed at the Indian River.

Chief Wildcat, or Coacoochie to his people, was one of the most formidable warriors of the Second Seminole War. When his mother, a black Seminole woman, was captured near Mosquito Inlet (New Smyrna), she shared that Spanish turtle fishermen brought in smuggled supplies for the Seminoles via the Florida Keys and delivered them to strategic positions along the area known today as the Treasure Coast.

JESUP'S PLEAS FOR WAR'S END

After the Battle of Loxahatchee in 1838, General Thomas Jesup realized that the Seminole force in Florida was severely depleted. Most of the Indians his men rounded up consisted of a few stubborn warriors, old men, women and children. According to Dr. Jacob Rhett Motte, a physician who traveled with the army, the Seminole prisoners were in a very poor state:

> *There were about four hundred of them and a great many negroes. Awaiting the will of their great father, the President. They might have been constantly seen wandering about our camp like domesticated animals; the men begging of everyone some tobacco; which being given; they smoked with a great deal of dignity; the squaws engaged in the less dignified employment of picking up the corn which our horses dropped from their mouths while eating; and which being sifted from the dirt, and pounded in mortars, was made into sofka; a dish the Indians devour with great gusto.*
> —*Jacob Rhett Motte,* Journey into the Wilderness, *1845*

Jesup was so distraught at the pointlessness of complete Indian removal from Florida that he wrote a letter to Secretary of War Poinsett:

> *It has been said that the national honor forbids any compromise with them…a band of naked savages, now beaten, broken, dispirited, and dispersed. I think those who believe so form a very low opinion of national honor.*

Thomas Sydney Jesup, 1837. *Library of Congress.*

Jesup went on to characterize the war itself as a "reckless waste of blood and treasure" and asserted that if the United States allowed the Seminoles a few years on a miserable tract of land, they would soon request emigration themselves. All it would take would be for the War Department to not identify success solely with an unyielding drive to subjugate the Seminoles. His pleas were ignored by the government, and the Seminole Indian Wars endured for many more years.

SLAVE TRADE ACT OF 1808

In response to international pressure, the United States passed legislation regarding the slave trade. The U.S. Prohibition of the Slave Trade Act went into effect on January 1, 1808. This law made it illegal to import slaves into the United States from other countries. It did nothing, however, to curtail the domestic slave trade that had been in use for hundreds of years. This proved to be a boon to slave traders and smugglers for nearly fifty years—until the Civil War. The law was, for the most part, ignored by plantation owners, and the number of slaves imported into Cuban slave markets from Africa jumped from one thousand in 1809 to fourteen thousand in 1811. Most of these slaves were introduced to the United States on the west coast of Florida, but many were brought in from the Caribbean along the isolated east coast beaches of the Treasure Coast. Slavery was the basis for the country's economic partnership with Cuba and the Bahamas for much of the nineteenth century. Today, commonly held perceptions concerning Caribbean piracy in the early nineteenth century often discount the fact that many of the early slave traders were American seamen and frontiersmen intent on purchasing slave cargoes from Cuban slave smugglers en route to the United States. In those wild times, slave trading was very lucrative and appealed to a wide variety of characters.

Journey of Misery

One can only imagine the confusion and terror that the newly captured African slaves must have endured after being brutally seized and imprisoned by slave hunters from other tribes, and then marched up the Congo to be stored in a crude barracoon on the river. They would then be placed in chains and forced onto dirty, unsanitary slave ships on which they would endure the grueling, long journey through the Middle Passage to Cuba.

Several of their people would perish along the way from the extremely harsh conditions, their wasted bodies thrown into the churning waters of the Atlantic. When they finally landed on some unknown port or obscure beach on the coast of Cuba, they would be herded off to be once again confined in crude quarters on one of the many brutal sugar plantations. After an undetermined length of time, they would be abruptly marched back to another port or beach to be loaded onto a slave dealer's ship for re-exportation. Another horrible sea journey would follow. Often, the slave ships would be attacked by pirates, who would board the ship and roughly transfer them to their own cargo holds. Either way, a short journey up the Atlantic coast would follow. They would then land at an isolated port on the east coast of Florida, where squalid quarters once again greeted them:

THE AFRICANS OF THE SLAVE BARK "WILDFIRE."—[FROM OUR OWN CORRESPONDENT.]

THE SLAVE DECK OF THE BARK "WILDFIRE," BROUGHT INTO KEY WEST ON APRIL 30, 1860.—[FROM A DAGUERREOTYPE.]

The Africans of the slave bark *Wildfire. Library of Congress.*

large, strategic slave depots located at places like Amelia Island, Mosquito Lagoon and the Indian River. At the humiliating and denigrating slave auctions, they would be purchased by rough, hard slave traders, who would then march them through the winding, swampy trails of the Florida swamps northward toward whichever cotton, sugar or rice plantation awaited their labors in the Deep South. This journey, from Africa to the United States and all points between, lasted anywhere from a few weeks to a few months. This was profitable for the slave traders at the time. A single successful slave journey from Cuba to the U.S. coast could net as much as $200,000, a vast fortune for the time. In 1846, Ezra Seaman, prominent economist and theorist, estimated that over 100,000 slaves were illegally imported to the United States from 1830 to 1840 alone.

BLACK SEMINOLES

In the early eighteenth century, many black refugees and slaves sought refuge in what was then Spanish Florida. Once in the territory, they encountered the villages and towns of the powerful Seminole Indians. They reached Florida through a variety of means, such as escape from southern plantations, slave ships or exploring parties or liberation by Spanish masters. Although they were often introduced into the tribes as slaves of the chiefs, the black Seminoles eventually found an identity of their own, quickly forging a strategic alliance with their native captors. While some individual black Seminoles were fugitive slaves, as a community, they were known

Negro Abraham.

Abraham, a prominent black Seminole warrior and leader. *Library of Congress.*

as maroons, a term that describes free and quasi-free blacks who escaped to the wilderness in the New World to create their own societies. Maroon communities were found all over the New World, especially in Brazil and the Caribbean. The black Seminoles were by far the most extensive maroon community in North America.

Even though these escaped slaves were considered "stolen property" by the whites to the north, the truth was more complex. Even though the Seminoles adopted the European concept of slaves as property, theirs was more a system of indentured servitude in which the blacks were given immense freedoms and allowed to create their own settlements outside of the Seminole towns. The runaway blacks were extremely valuable to the tribe for many reasons. They could speak the language of the whites and were excellent at farming, animal husbandry and building houses. They were also fierce fighters, many of them eventually rising to the level of *tustenuggee*, or war chief. Black Seminole warriors were often the most feared foes of the U.S. Army. One reason for this was that they had everything to lose if they were taken prisoner by the whites. If captured, they would be sent to plantations in places like Georgia or South Carolina to be slaves, even if they were born and raised in one of the black Seminole towns in Florida:

> *The two races, the negro and the Indians, are rapidly approximating; they are identified in interests and feelings; and I have ascertained that at the battle of Wahoo, a negro, the property of a Florida planter, was one of the most distinguished of the leaders, and I have learned that the depredations committed on the plantations east of the St. John's were perpetrated by the plantation negroes, headed by an Indian negro, John Caesar, since killed, and aided by some six or seven vagabond Indians, who had no character among their people as warriors. Should the Indians remain in this territory, the negroes among them will form a rallying point for runaway negroes from the adjoining states; and should they remove the fastnesses of the country would be immediately occupied by negroes.*
> —General Thomas Sydney Jesup, dispatch to Secretary of War Poinsett from the Florida Territory, June 16, 1837

After the Battle of Loxahatchee in January 1838, General Jessup gathered several captured black Seminoles at Fort Jupiter and organized them for removal to Fort Pike, Louisiana, where they would then be transported overland to the reservation in the Oklahoma Territory. He kept records of the blacks that he took prisoner and listed who their "owners" were. The relationship between the Seminoles and the black Seminoles was a complicated one. Many Seminoles refused to immigrate to the Oklahoma Territory without their "black brothers."

THE SEARCH FOR HELP ON ANDROS ISLAND

As early as the year 1812, the Seminole leaders knew that they would eventually have to seek refuge somewhere where they would be free of persecution by the whites. They were so concerned about the future that they sent one of their chiefs, Kenhadjo, to New Providence Island (Nassau) to ask for help from the British, whom they believed were sympathetic to their plight. Kenhadjo and his party made the hazardous journey across the ocean in sail-rigged canoes. When they arrived, the British representatives, who were still reeling from their stunning defeat by the United States, refused their pleas, stating that they had to honor the recent treaty that had ended the War of 1812. The Indians were then promptly led back to the Eastern Seaboard of the United States. Two years passed before another contingent of Seminoles arrived in New Providence with another plea for assistance. They carried with them a "Certificate of Good Conduct" from the British government for their contributions during the war. Much to their disappointment, they were once again rebuffed, returning to the United States empty-handed.

In 1821, the black Seminoles began to realize that their days were numbered in Florida. A contingent of them embarked on a boat from Key Biscayne, then known as Cape Florida, headed for the Bahamas. Their leaders must have realized the futility of appealing to the British for help, because rather than making New Providence their destination, they headed for the northwest tip of remote Andros Island. There they set up camp and established the community of Red Bays. Over the next sixteen years, over 150 black Seminoles left from various ports along the Florida coast in small boats, risking their lives in the treacherous crossing to Andros to find refuge in Red Bays. As time passed, they received some assistance from the sympathetic captains of British wrecking ships, many of whom had already transported the Seminoles to New Providence for negotiations with the British government years earlier. When things were at their bleakest for the black Seminoles, these captains provided them transport to Andros, where they found salvation. Many of these brave fugitives did not survive the journey. Their names are lost to history, but the struggle of the black Seminoles should always be remembered as an essential part of Florida's torrid history.

RED BAYS

Andros Island, largest in the Bahamas chain, is still a rugged archipelago covered with limestone hardscrabble, skinny pines, palmetto bushes, blue-hole caves and giant land crabs. The countryside is filled with tall straight pines and rough limestone rock ground. The largest of the Bahamian islands, it has the third-largest barrier reef in the world. Its land mass is made up of small islands interconnected by mangrove-filled estuaries and low swamps. It has three main sections: North Andros, Mangrove Cay and South Andros.

In the old days, it was only a three-day dugout canoe ride from South Florida across the Gulf Stream. The Seminole connection to the island's residents remained relatively unknown to the world until the mid-1930s when ethnomusicologist Alan Lomax wrote about the "Seminole Negroes" and recorded a song sung by a Mr. Bowlegs, a resident of Andros Island. Over three hundred descendants of the original black Seminoles live and work there today, as they have for over two hundred years. Familiar names like Bowlegs are common, and Seminole traditions are still prevalent in their culture, thanks to a few diligent teachers who strive to keep the history alive. Most of the residents make their living as sponge divers, fishermen, wood and fabric workers and especially basket weavers. The baskets they manufacture are so well made that they are sought after all over the world.

The community is dotted with small wooden sea cottages and houses of varying design, each one in varying stages of completion, some with families of six living in two rooms. Despite the sparse conditions and the trials and tribulations of island living, the people of Red Bays are happy and content with their home.

6

Smuggling on the Treasure Coast, 1845~65

I n the mid-1800s, the east coast of Florida was an empty and formidable place. The Indians who had lived there for thousands of years were gone, decimated by a combination of disease, slavery and a constant battle with the Spanish, and the coastline was desolate, save for a few Seminole Indians who frequented the area. With its newly minted statehood as of 1845, the fledgling government of Florida sought to organize its boundaries. On a map, it's easy to see that the area known today as the Treasure Coast is not far from the Bahamas, especially at Jupiter, which is only 71 miles from West End. The Jupiter Inlet there has long been an active place for all sorts of activity, both legitimate and illicit. There are a series of reefs located in the shallow waters a short distance from shore that made travel treacherous for any ships that ventured in too close as they made their way north along the Bahama Channel. If they were traveling south, they had to navigate between the north-flowing current of the Gulf Stream and land, this route often putting them in proximity to the jagged reefs. They would often wreck near the coastline, the survivors stranded on the desolate beach as they waited for rescuers from Key West to come save them. Salvage law of the time was quite clear, stating that the rescuers had to provide for the survivors before they could start their business of wrecking the stricken ships.

After surviving a harrowing shipwreck, the hapless victims' salvation would eventually arrive in the form of wreckers from the southernmost island who would first perform the required rescue, then salvage their damaged vessel for the standard 50 percent cut of what they had been transporting. This happened so often that the U.S. government formed the Light House Board

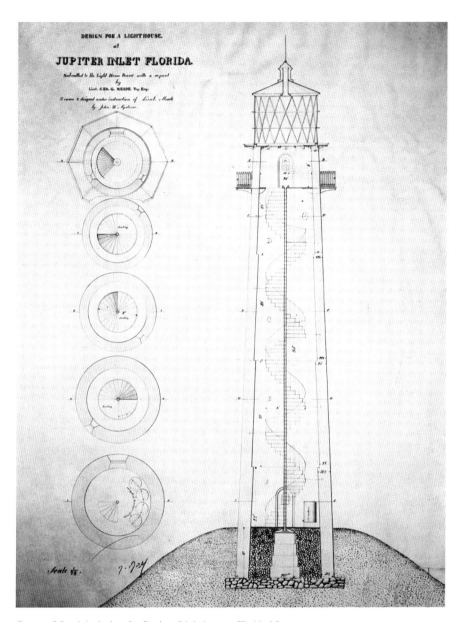

George Meade's design for Jupiter Lighthouse. *Florida Memory.*

to oversee the construction of several beacons along the lonely Florida coast to help captains navigate the dangerous reefs. The board's Seventh District, headed by a young engineer named George Meade, later of Gettysburg fame, set to designing a structure at the fickle Jupiter Inlet.

Jupiter Light, Seminole Indians on dock. *Jackson, William Henry, 184—1942, photographer, Detroit Publishing Company, publisher, Library of Congress.*

With a budget of $35,000, Meade stated that the lighthouse would be erected and operating in one year. The engineer failed to anticipate the hardships involved in the project. In those days, this area of Florida was an extremely difficult and remote place to construct any building, let alone a beacon 108 feet tall on a 48-foot-high natural sand hill. Workers had to contend with the blistering heat, the suffocating humidity, black clouds of insects in the summer months and the nearly impossible logistics of getting supplies through the too-shallow inlet. When Mother Nature decided to close the inlet with sand and silt, the area around the construction site became a stagnant pool festering with mosquito larvae. Many of the workers contracted a form of malaria dubbed "Jupiter Fever." Due to numerous delays and setbacks, the project's funding was re-appropriated, and construction was abandoned. Miraculously, the government soon located more funding, and the lighthouse was finally completed. The official lighting ceremony was performed on July 10, 1860. The project took nearly seven years and $60,000 to complete. It seemed that the area was just too desolate and unpopulated for a concentrated effort.

THE CIVIL WAR COMES TO
SOUTH FLORIDA'S EAST COAST

After the bombing of Fort Sumter on April 12, 1861, the country erupted into a bloody and violent struggle. In an act of desperation, the North established a blockade of all the ports on thousands of miles of U.S. coastline to "choke off" the South. The Anaconda Plan authorized a series of blockades that stretched, on the East Coast, all the way from Hampton Roads, Virginia, to Key West, Florida. It also covered from the Florida Keys to Brownsville, Texas, along the entire Gulf of Mexico. This was an immense territory to police and required a major effort and commitment of military resources to fully put into motion.

During the Civil War, the southeast coast of Florida remained sparsely populated, mostly due to the unforgiving heat and brutal conditions. At the outbreak of hostilities, men loyal to the Confederacy disabled the Jupiter Lighthouse, and it remained dark for the duration of the war. For these reasons, the area known today as the Treasure Coast was an ideal

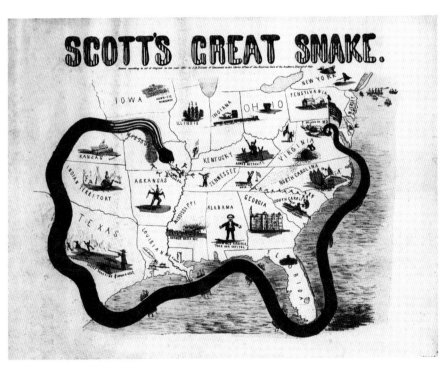

"Scott's Great Snake" General Winfield Scott's Anaconda Plan to choke the South with blockades. *Library of Congress.*

stretch of land for smuggling, especially under the cloak of darkness. The Northern blockades meant hardship for everyone, so the covert smuggling of all items classified as "contraband" became very popular. Many of the original "blockade runners" were Confederate sympathizers and British entrepreneurs out to make as much money as possible. There was a huge market for salt, turpentine and cotton in England, so the profit margin was high for the crafty individual who could get these things through the barrier. The navy had to handle the situation with captured British smugglers carefully so as not to create an adverse international incident. The smugglers knew this and would brazenly take chances that they would not normally take to get these valuable goods through without detection.

The Florida coast was still largely untamed, so the navy was based in the busy port of Key West. There were six gunboats assigned with the sole task of policing the waters from Cape Canaveral to Jupiter Inlet. The small war vessels, the USS *Sagamore*, *Gem of the Sea*, *Roebuck*, *Honeysuckle*, *Beauregard* and *Union*, were commissioned with the task of patrolling every inch of coastline within those boundaries. Just to put into perspective how ambitious the plan was, try to imagine the logistics involved in implementing it. There were hundreds of miles of seemingly endless mangrove-lined coastline with countless islands, coves, inlets and creeks to navigate. There was no Miami, Fort Lauderdale or West Palm Beach, so the dark, isolated coastline was ideal for performing illicit activities without detection. Despite this difficulty, navy records show that there were no fewer than forty-seven vessels that were captured smuggling goods in the waters of the Treasure Coast, nearly half of them caught near Jupiter. The largest inlet in the area, Jupiter Inlet was a hotbed of illegal smuggling activity and the best place for the blockade runners to "make a run for it" out to the open sea.

Most of the crafts that the navy used to enforce the blockades were known as "90-day gunboats." These were steam-powered vessels with shallow drafts that could supposedly be completely assembled and ready for battle in ninety days. Though this lofty goal was sometimes hard to achieve, the navy cranked out an impressive twenty-three of them in five months. Each one was 159 feet long, had a 28-foot beam and displaced about 507 tons. Even though they were not large ships, they were armed with many guns, including howitzers, several cannons and a large one-inch smoothbore.

The mire of countless creeks and tributaries afforded excellent hiding places, giving the smugglers a definite advantage over the navy gunboats that hunted them. Traveling through these vine-choked passages was

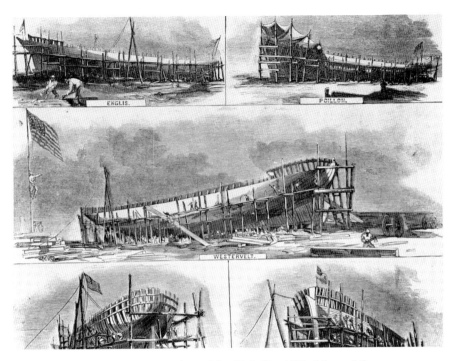

"90-Day" gunboats under construction at New York City, 1861. *Library of Congress.*

always a struggle because it was easy to get hung up on the thick ropes of vegetation. Snakes, rats and other creatures would fall onto the decks of the boats, adding to the near-unbearable conditions that the gunboat crews already had to endure. Sickness from the relentless heat and humidity was always a danger, not to mention the hordes of blood-sucking pests that relentlessly preyed on the men. In those days, mosquitos moved across the mangrove swamps and prairies of South Florida in thick black clouds, and the tiny, voracious insects known as "no see ums" could nearly drive a person insane. One of the gunboats that cruised the waters of the Treasure Coast, the USS *Honeysuckle*, experienced a yellow fever epidemic so devastating that it wiped out nearly the entire crew. It was forced to return to Key West so the men could recuperate.

Another challenge for the gunboat crews was dealing with the long periods of inactivity. The gunboats would often go for weeks or even months without seeing any blockade runners. Most of the real action of the war was occurring far to the north. It was a good feeling when an illegal salt operation or a hidden marina was discovered and destroyed.

African Americans played a large role in the success of the navy gunboats. Escaped slaves often knew the terrain well and guided the crews to many Confederate camps. The navy was integrated much earlier than any of the other services. The main reason for this were the confined quarters of the men on boats and the extreme difficulty of the day-to-day tasks. If the man next to you was an able seaman and hard worker, he was a great asset to any sailing ship, regardless of the color of his skin or the language he spoke. Great numbers of African American men joined the navy and served honorably in anti-smuggling operations.

There were many reasons why the navy was so diligent in catching renegade smuggling vessels, but one stands out. The gunboat crews had a strong incentive to apprehend any boat they could. At that time, any contraband vessels of war apprehended in the Florida waters were confiscated and transported to Key West, where they would be sold in the large maritime auctions in Mallory Square. The money generated by this would often go to the officers and crew themselves. The rewards from this maritime commerce were sometimes very lucrative.

In 1862, the gunboat *Gem of the Sea* captured and destroyed the blockade runner *Anne* near the Jupiter Inlet, dumping its massive England-bound cargo of seventy-six barrels of salt into the sea. The following year, it seized the Confederate blockade runner *Inez* in the Indian River. *Inez*'s cargo of salt suffered the same fate as the *Anne*'s.

The USS *Beauregard* was originally a Confederate vessel that was commandeered early in the war. Its original builders and crew would have been very unhappy to hear that it apprehended eleven Confederate blockade runners along the coast of Florida during the war years.

USS *ROEBUCK*

The Confederate blockade runners were very familiar with the reputation of the USS *Roebuck*. It was a formidable, heavily gunned clipper ship with a crew of sixty-nine men under the leadership of Captain John Sherrill. When it arrived at Jupiter, it immediately started to inflict damage on the blockade runners, seizing the British vessel *Ringdom* with a full load of salt, cotton and coffee bound for the Bahamas. It then took the *Maria Louise* near Jupiter Inlet and the *Suzan*, which was converted to a patrol boat later used to cruise the coast of Jupiter Island. Other victims of the USS *Roebuck*

The gunboat *Planter*, run out of Charleston, South Carolina. *Library of Congress*.

were the British ships *Young Racer* and the *Mary* and the Confederate ships *Caroline* and *Eliza*. It was credited with many more conquests farther south as the end of the war drew nearer and the noose around the neck of the South grew tighter.

USS *UNION*

The USS *Union* was a massive steam powered ship that was first utilized as a fleet gunboat tender before it was converted to a warship in 1864. When it was put into service, its crew apprehended and seized two vessels near the Jupiter Inlet; the Confederate *Caroline* and the Havana-based *Emma*. After *Emma*'s capture, the navy towed the craft all the way back to Key West, where it was put up for auction.

USS *SAGAMORE*

The USS *Sagamore* was the most successful of the gunboats that patrolled the area during the Civil War years, taking a great toll on smugglers. The *Sagamore*'s job was to lead a continuous "search and destroy" mission on Confederate shipyards that had been covertly constructed along Florida's coast. Constant surveillance of the coastline under harsh South Florida conditions was a never-ending job that required a rugged breed of man to do it properly. These individuals had to be extremely tough, resourceful and familiar with the coast of Florida. The men charged with the leadership of the USS *Sagamore* were Captain Earl English and Master Mate Henry Crane. Crane was a strong Florida boy who had served in both the First and Second Seminole Indian Wars, so he was already familiar with the guerrilla warfare and resourceful tactics that had to be learned by the U.S. Navy during those turbulent years. Under his wily guidance, the USS *Sagamore* would prove to be the most successful anti-smuggling gunboat of the war in Florida's waters.

In 1862, the USS *Sagamore* was still serving in the northwest region of Florida. There, it captured the Confederate *Apalachicola* and destroyed some key saltworks at St. Andrews Bay. *Sagamore* was then transferred to the east coast of Florida, where it continued to wreak havoc on the blockade runners. Not long after its arrival, Crane and his crew overtook and commandeered the English schooner *By George* near the Indian River Inlet. In 1863, they seized the British ship *Julia* ten miles north of Jupiter Inlet, just off the coast of present-day Stuart, Florida. The *Sagamore* then apprehended the Confederate ship *Pride* in the river near Jupiter, the victorious raiders dumping the immensely valuable cargo of 188 bushels of salt into the water. The *Sagamore* then paid a visit to the abandoned Jupiter lighthouse, where her crew found a hidden cache of 150 gallons of whale oil and 200 bushels

On deck of U.S. gunboat *Hunchback. Library of Congress.*

of salt. Later that month, they discovered 45 sacks of salt at a place called Couch's Bar near the Jupiter Inlet, then seized 7 bales of cotton in the Jupiter Narrows. Two days after that, they returned to the still abandoned lighthouse and discovered 58 more sacks of salt waiting for a covert retrieval by a smuggler. Then came the *Sagamore*'s most significant victory: Crane and his men discovered a fully operating Confederate shipyard near the Indian River Inlet, which they promptly destroyed.

One can only wonder how many more undocumented violent encounters occurred out in the ocean during those turbulent years. The efforts of the Union blockade gunboats and their crews will always be remembered for their great sacrifice and commitment to the Union cause. They not only made monumental contributions to the war effort but also to the rich history of Florida's Treasure Coast.

7

Florida's Whiskey Pirates and Smugglers

Before the 1920s, the area known today as the Treasure Coast was much different than it is today. At that time, Martin County didn't even yet exist, so the rural communities of Hobe Sound, Stuart, Salerno and Jensen Beach fell under the jurisdiction of northern Palm Beach County. Unlike other Florida locations, the area was still so remote and unpopulated that it was largely avoided by law enforcement officials, who were reluctant to make the journey into the wilderness. Its residents were a mixture of rough commercial fisherman, shady business entrepreneurs, criminals, railroad workers and rugged homesteaders looking for a new start.

THE GREAT FLORIDA LAND BOOM

Considered a rural, lawless backwater, the area's main industry was fishing and land speculation. The country's economy was on the rise, so many Americans were looking to buy real estate in "paradise." The great Florida land boom was in full swing, with real estate agents from northern states touting the swampy, forested land as an "Eden-like" paradise available for a reasonable price. Also, the advent of the automobile made it possible for young families to venture to places like Florida. This was the beginning of a new era of the middle-class family. The "tin can tourists" were people of modest means who traveled to Florida in cars or trucks carrying tents

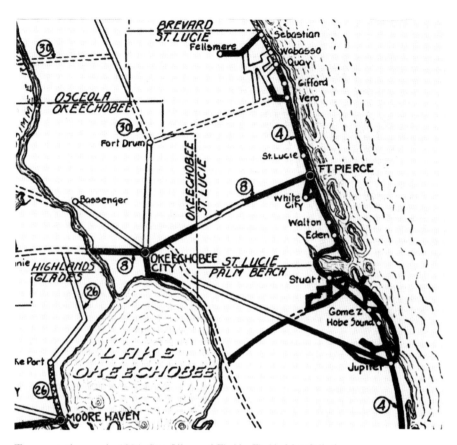

Transportation roads, 1924. *State Library of Florida, Florida Map Collection.*

and camping equipment. They got their name from the extra gas and oil cans they carried with them. They were not wealthy Americans with the sole intent of purchasing land but vacationing families looking for the sandy beaches. They were the precursors of the "mobile home invasion" of the 1940s and '50s.

Millions of people were caught up in the idea that extreme wealth was only one smart investment away. It didn't matter if you didn't have the cash; mountains of credit were easy to obtain. Florida's state government borrowed tons of money at high-interest rates to make improvements to roads and other investments that would help bring more people to the Sunshine State. Newspapers touted the exploits of land investors that doubled, or even tripled, their investments overnight. Almost two-thirds of land speculation deals were made by mail, with the buyers never actually coming to inspect the sites they had purchased. The real estate agents would employ "binder boys" to meet the clients that did come. These were young, intelligent men that were willing to take a small down payment from investors and offer a thirty-day "binder" for the balance. They would offer to take a prospective client on a golf outing or to play a game of tennis to emphasize what a solid investment they were about to make. Even though there was not much actual cash available for them, there was a high amount of prestige involved for a young man who would soon be coming into so much wealth.

Around the year 1925, cracks began to show in the burgeoning Florida economy. As investors in the North noticed poor returns on their properties, New York newspapers began to shout out headlines condemning the "Florida sham real estate deals." Land prices had reached their peak, and buyers began to shy away. Owners began to sell off their property. Residents of towns and villages saw fewer and fewer new people moving in, so they began to panic about the loans they had taken out for improvements. Resentment in rural communities grew, and there was an increase in violent activity against black workers from hate groups like the Ku Klux Klan. The year 1926 brought a terrible hurricane that demolished many oceanside towns. This pulled the rug out from under any favorable view of Florida land purchases. Two years later, in 1928, another vicious hurricane raged over Lake Okeechobee, destroying the poorly constructed dikes and killing as many as 2,800 people, most of them black cane workers and their families, in the western communities of Belle Glade, Canal Point and Clewiston. The storm created such a high wave of water that several bodies of drowned victims were later found hanging from trees. The news of this disaster spread quickly all around the country, thus sealing Florida's fate. The state experienced the crushing weight of the Great Depression years before the rest of the country did. However, there was one business that thrived in the Sunshine State no matter what happened.

Temperance Comes to Florida

Alcohol has always been extremely popular in America. For hundreds of years, its citizens have depended on it for nearly everything—from recreational use to medicine and keeping babies from crying at night. The great Benjamin Franklin, a man who was known to imbibe quite frequently, summed up his own thoughts on the matter: "In wine there is wisdom, in beer there is Freedom, and in water there is bacteria."

It was indeed hard to imagine that society could function without it. Alcohol usage was so deeply ingrained in the public psyche that if one did not choose to drink, he or she would sometimes be viewed in a negative light. Winston Churchill once quipped, "Never trust a man who doesn't drink."

Of course, alcohol had its dark side as well. Alcoholism was rampant, and many men and women would spend their entire lives in a fog. Domestic abuse was common, as were financial losses and total ruination. Booze was also blamed for a sharp increase in violent crime. Shortly after the end of the great Civil War, the Woman's Christian Temperance Union was formed. This organization introduced anti-alcohol education programs in schools and pushed hard for reform for many years. In 1907, Georgia became the first state to ban the sale of alcohol. The "dry laws" soon passed to many other states like Virginia, Mississippi and North Carolina. When the Eighteenth Amendment passed in 1919, the entire country was forced to follow suit. The only two states that absolutely refused to ratify the amendment were Connecticut and Rhode Island.

Section 1. After one year from the ratification of this article the manufacture, sale, or transportation of intoxicating liquors within, the importation thereof into, or the exportation thereof from the United States and all the territory subject to the jurisdiction thereof for beverage purposes is hereby prohibited. Section 2. The Congress and the several States shall have concurrent power to enforce this article by appropriate legislation. Section 3. This article shall be inoperative unless it shall have been ratified as an amendment to the Constitution by the legislatures of the several States, as provided in the Constitution, within seven years from the date of the submission hereof to the States by the Congress. Eighteenth Amendment to the Constitution, ratified on January 16, 1919.

In October 1919, the Volstead Act passed through Congress, which provided enforcement legislation for the Eighteenth Amendment. When the manufacture and sale of alcohol became illegal in January 1920, the thirst for it did not. Almost immediately, a nationwide black market opened to fill the void. The gangsters pounced on this opportunity for financial gain and quickly began to reap the huge benefits of "filling a need" to a very thirsty behemoth. There were four main areas in the United States where the largest amount of liquor smuggling occurred: Chicago, Detroit, New

York City, and Florida. Chicago and Detroit became mighty kingdoms that relied on transport by trucking over land, but New York and Florida had a definite advantage over them. They had the sea. At that time in history, Florida was sparsely populated, so it was relatively easy to smuggle illegal booze in almost anywhere along the 1,350 miles of wild coastline. The Treasure Coast was ideal for smuggling due to its proximity and ready access to the Bahamas.

Prohibition did not exist in England, so its Caribbean islands became the home of warehouses where illegal booze was stored for eventual sales to American liquor smugglers. The settlement of West End on Grand Bahama Island sported nine operating liquor warehouses, all waiting to supply the rumrunners whenever they came. This provided an incredible financial boost to the economy. The seemingly endless streams of cash enabled the locals to make vast improvements to the island's infrastructure. Grand Bahama was soon importing millions of quarts of whiskey a year, supplying illegal booze for the entire Atlantic Seaboard of the United States. To its south lay the island of Bimini, where huge barges were set up to be manned twenty-four hours a day to service its "customers."

WILD TIMES INDEED

During the turbulent years of Prohibition, it was very easy to procure illegal booze in any of the communities located along the Treasure Coast. The term "moonshine" usually pertained to any homemade liquor on which no taxes had been paid. You could buy it any gas station or store simply by asking the right question. The rule was "anywhere but the bank." Coastal Martin, St. Lucie and Brevard Counties were the prime destination for those looking to trade with the English warehouses in the Bahamas. Rumrunning was an extremely lucrative business. Remote coves and inlets, like the tiny Manatee Pocket in tiny Salerno, were perfect spots to bring in illegal booze at night. These small locations were far from the prying eyes of customs officials, who were busy in more populated areas like West Palm Beach to the south, or Fort Pierce to the north. If the rumrunners could navigate the sixty- or seventy-mile trip to West End in their speedboats without incident, they could purchase a whole case of six quarts of whiskey for around ten dollars from one of the crude shanty-like warehouses along the Bahamian waterfront. Then came the often-harrowing trip back to the mainland in the dark of night, their boats loaded to the waterline with contraband. Once safely back on the mainland, they could then sell each individual bottle for four or five dollars each. The runners themselves were often not the original buyers but transported the booze for others. Many men and women got very rich during these wild times.

It wouldn't surprise any resident living along the shore to find a broken and battered boat that had washed up on the beach looking as if it had endured a pounding storm at sea, its bottom filled with broken and empty bottles, the stench of booze filling the morning air. Sometimes there would be bullet holes in its worn hull and the conspicuous absence of an owner's registration or information anywhere onboard. The locals would spend a few minutes speculating about what had transpired the night before, but no report would be made to the law. The average Florida residents of that time did not think much of the Volstead Act and tended to look the other way when they saw something fishy. Lots of local fisherman took up the "night-time trade" to help make ends meet, and many an uncle or brother lost their lives in condemned vessels such as these.

The rural areas of today's Martin and St. Lucie Counties are dotted with old still sites in which hundreds of gallons of illegal moonshine were manufactured. All through the 1920s and early 1930s, bootleg whiskey was manufactured in the backwoods and swamps of the coastal communities. It wasn't uncommon for law enforcement to raid over thirty stills a year. An exasperated Martin County sheriff made a statement warning against the unsanitary habits of some of the bootleggers:

> *"I would not drink a glassful of some of the liquor we have seized for $1000.00," the Sheriff declared. "Most of it is matured by the addition of potash. Some of the mash is allowed to ferment in holes hastily dug in the ground. It is not unusual to find cockroaches or rats in the fermented mash."*
> *—excerpt from the* Stuart News, *article by Roberta Crawford, 1975*

Smugglers "custom fitted" the trunks of their automobiles with false bottoms and had their axles equipped with extra springs so the rear end didn't hang too low when full of booze. Moonshiners working in the woods would wear hooved "cow shoes" to cover their tracks and make it look as if cattle were grazing in the area. Pigs that were slaughtered and gutted for market were stuffed with bottles and crudely sewn up for transport. It seemed as if entire towns along the coast were involved in the illegal trade.

Florida bootleggers in front of a crude still during Prohibition. *Steve Carr Collection*.

Since barrooms were illegal, private homes were often utilized for the consumption of booze and general partying. One such speakeasy, located in the tiny hamlet of Hobe Sound, was raided and yielded three hundred bottles of homemade liquor and over nine gallons of moonshine.

There is one memorable story that occurred in 1927 in Salerno, a small fishing community just south of Stuart. It was early in the morning, and a fisherman and part-time rumrunner was preparing to offload his cargo of illegal booze onto a small dock in the Manatee Pocket. Suddenly, a careless boater came barreling in from the inlet, his motor roaring loudly as he turned in a great arc, creating a huge wake. The rumrunning fisherman panicked and hurriedly started his own motor and immediately high-tailed it toward the inlet, certain that his activities had been discovered by a revenue agent. As he fled, he threw his valuable goods overboard, one burlap bag at a time, all the way from the Pocket to Rocky Point, over a mile. Word spread through the small, tight-knit community quickly, and before long the entire town was down along the banks of the Pocket with their fishing rods, each hoping to snag one of the "hams."

Rumrunners and bootleggers sometimes stole from one another other. There is one well-known tale about an old local who was caught stealing whiskey from a hidden cache on the North Fork of the river. After roughing him up, the angry bootleggers decided to give him a ride to West End in the Bahamas in their seaplane. Well, he made it *halfway* to the Bahamas. The old man was never seen again.

In another story, a trapper was in the process of relocating some hidden booze he had found in a cabbage palm hammock near Peck's Lake in Hobe Sound to another location for safekeeping. Just as he was making the last trip in his canoe, the bootleggers showed up. Understandably peeved, they politely asked him where he had stashed their booze. Apparently not satisfied with the old-timer's answer, they roughly grabbed him by his long hair and forced his head under the cold water. Just as it seemed that he would drown, they pulled him up, letting him splutter and gasp for air for a few seconds. They would then dunk him again. After several minutes of this, the trapper passed out cold. He woke up several hours later, dazed and scared, in the bootleggers' West Palm Beach hideout. The rough, hard men kept him tied up there for a week, constantly interrogating him about the whereabouts of their pilfered booze. Exasperated at the trapper's stubborn nature, they finally informed him that they had endured his presence long enough and that they were going to drive him out into the woods and shoot him dead. As they were leaving, the trapper kicked the door open and fled the car, running down the middle of Clematis Street like a madman in his underwear. When he was safely away from his captors, he sent word to them where he had hidden their booze.

THE REAL MCCOY

Lieutenant Commander Perkins of the *Seneca* stared at the vessel before him. Earlier that day, his watchman had discovered the schooner *Tomoka* sitting placidly at anchor, three miles out in the ocean. It had been a long day, and Commander Perkins was ready to make his move. He quietly gave his orders, and his bosun, along with thirteen sailors, quickly took to a smaller boat and began discreetly making their way to the stern of the *Tomoka*. They pulled alongside it, quietly climbing aboard. One of the bootlegger crew members discovered the unwanted intruders and immediately shouted out to the others. Mayhem instantly ensued as the Coast Guard sailors leapt into

William McCoy on deck of the *Tomoka*. *The Mariners' Museum Collection.*

action. There was a furious fistfight, with men cursing and grunting loudly as they viciously pounded one another. The close-quarters brawl soon spilled onto the slippery deck. As Commander Perkins tensely watched from the *Seneca*, he noticed that the *Tomoka* was slowly turning east toward the open sea. When he realized what was happening, he angrily ordered his gunner to fire a warning shot. The *Tomoka*'s captain, a man named William McCoy, had made the brash decision to flee, even though the Coast Guard men were still fighting onboard his boat. Several four-inch shells burst from the *Seneca*'s guns with a resounding *boom*, passing directly over the bow of the *Tomoka*, creating huge geysers of spray as they hit the water and drenched the deck. This was apparently enough to convince the renegade captain to surrender.

William Frederick McCoy was born in Syracuse, New York, in 1877. His father was a brickmason who had been in the navy and participated in the Anaconda Plan, an attempt by the Union to strangle the South with a massive blockade of all the ports during the Civil War. For this reason, young William "Bill," his older brother Ben and his sister Violet were exposed to the sea at a very early age. Bill began working as an apprentice bricklayer to his father but spent most of his free time on the docks watching the vessels come in and leave on the Delaware River. He knew that bricklaying wasn't for him, so he worked hard at school, becoming a serious, intelligent young man who excelled at his studies. When he was old enough, he enrolled in the Pennsylvania Nautical School, then holding classes and training aboard the USS *Saratoga*. He proved to be an exemplary student, graduating at the very top of his class. Bill went on to serve aboard many different vessels, eventually ending up in Cuba, where he was promoted to first mate and quartermaster aboard the Peninsular and Oriental Steam Navigation Company Plant Line steamer USS *Olivette*. He was in Havana when the USS *Maine* exploded in the harbor in 1898.

After Bill completed his military service, he and his brother relocated to Holly Hill, Florida, where they opened a boatyard, charter and maritime freight business. The brothers were so adept at constructing yachts that they soon entertained a clientele of the rich and famous, including such names as Vanderbilt and Carnegie. They prospered in Holly Hill for many years, but their business eventually fell victim to a changing Florida economy. World War I had ended, and the advent of the automobile and upgraded infrastructure provided more economic modes of travel and freight for a struggling, peacetime population. For this reason, the boat business suffered, and the McCoy brothers fell on hard times. Then came an event that changed Bill's future forever.

The Eighteenth Amendment of the U.S. Constitution effectively established the prohibition of alcoholic beverages in the United States by declaring the production, transport and sale of alcohol illegal. Bill was offered a job as captain of a schooner named the *Dorothy W* transporting liquor from a British warehouse in Nassau to Atlantic City for one hundred dollars a day. He didn't like the looks of the vessel or the questionable legality of the venture, so he declined, but the seed had been planted. Prohibition provided sailors like the McCoy brothers an irresistible chance to reverse their fortunes. It wasn't long before the boys went into the lucrative business of rumrunning.

Bill, seeing the writing on the wall, convinced his brother to sell all their assets in the boatyard. With $20,000 between them, they headed north to the busy port town of Gloucester, Massachusetts, where they discreetly made inquiries about purchasing a suitable vessel to use. According to Frederic F. Van de Water's biography of McCoy, *The Real McCoy*, it was on that trip that Bill first set his eyes on the boat of his dreams:

> Her name was Arethusa. *She seemed to ghost into the harbor's mouth under full sail. She was an aristocrat, a thoroughbred from her keel to her trucks. The sun turned her spread of canvas golden, and my throat was tight and stiff as she came walking up the harbor like a great lady entering a room.*

Financially strapped, the McCoy brothers settled on a ninety-foot fishing schooner, the *Henry L. Marshall*, and began to formulate plans. The boat could hold 1,500 wooden cases of whiskey, a case consisting of twelve bottles. Bill devised an ingenious storage plan to dramatically increase his capacity. He wrapped the bottles tightly in burlap and stacked them into triangles, three on the bottom, then two, then one. He would then interlock them, doubling the amount he could store. Bill called them called "burlocks." The other rumrunners referred to these as "hams," and the Coast Guard as "sacks."

His first commission was to transport a cargo from Nassau to Halifax, Nova Scotia. He stopped near New York and sold his cargo to contact boats that came out to meet him. Everything was legal because he stayed outside of the three-mile limit in international waters. On that single trip, the boys cleared $15,000. The McCoy brothers were officially hooked for life. This was the first of many of their commissions that helped their net worth grow exponentially. As soon as he could, Bill traveled back to Gloucester to purchase his dream boat, *Arethusa*, at a significantly discounted price of $42,000. The name *Arethusa* was already registered as a British vessel, so he

William McCoy's "Hams and Burlocks." *The Mariner's Museum Collection*.

changed the name to *Tomoka* after the river that ran through his hometown of Holly Hill, Florida. *Tomoka*'s hold could hold carry up to one thousand more cases than his old boat, so the brothers could now carry cargoes worth $50,000. Bill McCoy then embarked on a career of what most folks would call lawlessness, even though he was technically not breaking any laws.

Bill had an accomplice that he trusted more than any other associate, a black Newfoundland dog named Old Faithful. The animal never left his side for the entirety of his rumrunning career, sleeping on the cabin floor or in the same cot next to his beloved master. When the dog got too large, Bill had a separate cot built for him. Bill would often store large amounts of cash in his cabin but was never worried. "It was perfectly safe," he recalled. "If anyone had touched it, he would've had to kill or be killed."

Old Faithful was devoted to McCoy. When Bill had business to attend to in Bermuda, he left the dog on the boat. The next morning, one of the workers came to him and asked if he owned a big black dog. It seems that during the night, Old Faithful had jumped overboard and swam to the dock, found where Bill was staying and waited patiently right there by his window.

The brothers were soon dancing to the beat of a different drum. They were awash with success, with five boats in their armada. The three-mile limit, or "rum row," was like a circus by then, with visiting tourist boats, jazz bands playing and scores of small boats that had made the trip to purchase booze from "Bill McCoy, King of the Bootleggers." He had the reputation of being a straight shooter, refusing to double-deal anyone or water down his product, like many of the other rumrunners of that time. Customers looked to him as providing the "Real McCoy."

It is thought that over two million bottles of booze made their way to the U.S. coast during those years with the help of Bill McCoy. He had a signaling system that let customers know if he was open for business or not. He would place a bright electric light high on his mast as a signal. If the *Tomoka*, or any other supply ship, had the British colors flying, it meant that they should stay back. If there was no flag, it was safe to do business. Bill and Ben McCoy became famous, gaining the reputation of swashbuckling smugglers who lived dangerous lives.

Not everyone shared in the enthusiasm for men like Bill McCoy. U.S. Customs hated the fact that the rumrunners laughed in the face of the law. Most of the time, they couldn't even catch them in a chase, because the runners had equipped their boats with five-hundred-horsepower Liberty engines that could travel twice as fast as any of their cutters. The U.S. government began to step up its efforts dramatically, pumping millions of dollars into the Coast Guard fleet to help shut down the contact boats. Onshore, the Prohibition officers targeted boatbuilders and anyone supplying resources to the boat owners. The harassment took its toll, inflating the animosity between the boat industry and law enforcement. McCoy's old boat, the *Henry L. Marshall*, was captured and impounded when its intoxicated captain bragged about buying and selling illegal booze. Government agents claimed that any contact between the shore and the supply boats constituted an illegal act. The writing was on the wall. Indictments were processed, and the McCoys soon became wanted men.

Under pressure from the State Department, the British government agreed not to interfere with the apprehension of the McCoys. In November 1923, the *Seneca* sent a messenger boat out to check the *Tomoka*'s papers. When the revenuers insisted that Captain McCoy steer back toward Sandy Hook for a review, he refused. The *Seneca* was then ordered to either bring them in or sink *Tomoka* and McCoy. Realizing that his number was nearly up, Bill went below decks and paid his crew members, making tearful goodbyes. The inevitable confrontation with the *Seneca* and her men occurred, and McCoy ended up surrendering to authorities.

FOLK HERO

This set off a firestorm of publicity, with McCoy appearing as a folk hero to the underdog. His high moral character ended up paying great dividends. The arresting customs agent, Pete Sullivan, treated McCoy with the utmost respect. One year earlier, McCoy saved Sullivan's life in Nassau when he shielded him from some rough characters who had discovered the customs agent's true reason for being there. Sullivan hadn't forgot this act of selflessness, giving McCoy an impromptu tour of Washington. Many people, including several congressmen, wanted to meet the man who had thwarted the U.S. government in such a brash way for so long. In March 1925, William McCoy was found guilty and sentenced to nine months in prison. The sentence was so light that he was even allowed to leave the jail if he returned by 9:00 p.m. each night. There was a bit of a scandal when the warden took him to a prize fight. The warden was fired over the incident, and Bill was transferred to another jail. He was released on Christmas Day, only to discover that Old Faithful had died in his absence. He moved to Stuart, Florida, where he lived comfortably for the rest of his days. He died in 1948 at the age of seventy-one, and his ashes were spread over Stuart Inlet.

William McCoy, the King of the Bootleggers, will always be remembered as a straight-up opportunist who took advantage of a disastrously unpopular piece of legislation. He was the Real McCoy.

MARIE WAITE, "SPANISH MARIE"

Men were not the only rumrunners during Prohibition. After her husband was killed in a shootout with Coast Guard officials off the coast of Miami, Marie Waite inherited the family business, which consisted of running bootleg whiskey from Cuba to Key West and up the entire coast of Florida. A tall and beautiful woman, "Spanish Marie" proved to be no shrinking violet when it came to making money. She quickly built her reputation as a coldhearted professional who also had a broad knowledge of boats and trade routes. She ran her business from Havana, coordinating the movements of her armada of fifteen of the fastest and most well-armed boats in the business. Spanish Marie also had a reputation as a femme fatale, running through many men by plying her charms. It is said that her romances only lasted a few months before the poor man would end up missing, usually winding up in the ocean somewhere in the Caribbean. Spanish Marie did not like to leave loose ends.

The Coast Guard tried to apprehend her boats for years, but she evaded them by using multiple vessels—usually four at a time. Three of them would be carrying the booze cargo while the fourth carried the guns used to fend off the law enforcement boats. Spanish Marie tried to bribe them with cash as well. She applied all the technology she could, equipping her boats with radios. As time passed, the Coast Guard got wise to her tricks, and after a couple of banner years her empire slowly began to erode.

On March 12, 1928, Spanish Marie left her two babies sleeping at her home in Miami to personally verify a night delivery of over five thousand bottles of booze. She must have been anxious about this job because she had hired a pilot boat with the sole purpose of watching out for Coast Guard vessels near the spot on the coastline where the drop was supposed to occur. The boat's crew was then to contact the incoming delivery boat with a series of light signals to guide them in. To her dismay, she and her crew were caught unloading the illegal booze at the landing site in Coconut Grove near the city of Miami. Marie and ten of her associates were charged with the illegal transport of the huge cargo of alcohol. She then turned on the charm, becoming frantic about the welfare of her babies at home. In response to this situation, she was issued a bond of $500 and released. Marie never showed up for court the second day. Her attorney stated that she was at home, bedridden with "nervous prostration." When he was unable to produce a verification letter from her physician, the bond was raised to a whopping $3,000.

"Spanish Marie" Waite was never seen or heard from again. It is believed that she took her boats and left the country, probably heading back to her native Cuba. There are no records of her whereabouts. She had once more thwarted law enforcement with her personality and guile, forever joining the ranks of the infamous smugglers of Florida's Treasure Coast.

GERTRUDE "CLEO" LYTHGOE

There was no Prohibition in other countries, so more than a few foreigners were able to take advantage of the stilted laws. England benefited greatly from the proximity of its holdings near the United States' eastern coast. When the Eighteenth Amendment came to fruition in 1920, a young woman named Gertrude Lythgoe foresaw saw a golden opportunity. She moved to Nassau in the Bahamas and opened a liquor warehouse. For the next several years, she built up an infamous reputation as a hard-nosed, no-nonsense dealer you had to be careful with. Gertrude, or "Cleo" as many knew her, became the "Queen of the Bahamas" and the "Queen of Rum Row." She was an attractive woman, a fact that only added to her notoriety. Her business was incredibly successful, selling whiskey and other products to smaller dealers from the United States and working the "three-mile limit." She was a snappy dresser, good with a pistol, and had a smooth manner of speech.

Cleo Lythgoe was good friends with the infamous rumrunner William McCoy and did business with him for years. Her warehouses were the ideal place for McCoy to load his boats with his burlocks of whiskey, and the two became fast friends. Years later, McCoy described her fits of anger as "the breathtaking fury she could show." He respected her keen business sense and considered her to be one of the smartest, toughest women he had ever seen. He once witnessed her threaten to take a man's life because he spoke ill of her alcohol.

As time went by, Cleo Lythgoe battled a growing paranoia that she had a jinx on her. She began to think that it would only be a short amount of time

Gertrude (Cleo) Lythgoe with William McCoy aboard the *Tomoka*. *The Mariner's Museum Collection.*

before it took her business and, quite possibly, her life. In the year 1925, she abruptly gave up the smuggling business and went back to New York to live a quiet, comfortable life.

> *I just beat my jinx before it got me. I saw the signs when I was taking some whiskey from Nassau to another British island.*

Cleo Lythgoe moved out West and lived to the ripe old age of eighty-six. When she passed away, the island of Nassau flew its flags at half-mast in honor of the Queen.

"BIG AL" IN JUPITER

Did the infamous Chicago gangster Al Capone do business on Florida's Treasure Coast? According to a well-researched article written by historian Richard Procyk in 2005, it depends on who you ask. After the activation of the Volstead Act in 1920, many organized crime figures benefited greatly and came into huge amounts of money. Capone fought his way to the top of the crime syndicate by developing a reputation as a ruthless businessman and cold-blooded killer. He loved South Florida, moving to Palm Island in Miami to escape the frigid temperatures of the North. He quickly made his outsized reputation known by attracting all sorts of famous people and spending huge amounts of money. On many evenings during the season, residents reported seeing Capone and his gang members in Lake Worth when they came to see the fights.

Many believe that Capone bought land in western Jupiter, Florida, for a private, secluded hangout for his associates. There is no legal record of his ownership, but Capone would have never purchased land under his own name. Many locals reported seeing his gang members traveling in and out on old "Italian Farms Road." It is quite possible that the gangster would have chosen this area for a hideout. The rural location afforded great privacy for discreet meetings and activities. Only a couple of hours from the glaring lights of Miami, Capone and his gang would have had free reign for hunting, fishing, playing cards or possibly doling out frontier justice on some unfortunate "business associate." Also, the Jupiter Inlet was an ideal place in which to smuggle illegal booze. Compared to Miami, the place wasn't highly populated and was perfectly situated for quick trips from the Bahamas

Al Capone around 1935. *Public domain.*

under the cloak of night. People who lived near the inlet told stories of burlap and canvas sacks full of booze bottles washing up on the shoreline near the lighthouse and abandoned boats full of contraband liquor. The townsfolk would all line up to get their share of the booty, including members of local law enforcement.

There is one story that has been passed down through time and reflects the wildness of that period. It seems that a local grower was able to get involved in a transport deal with one of the mobsters from Italian Farms Road. He apparently made a deal with the devil to transport a load of illegal booze to Philadelphia on his trailer. The booze was to be disguised by oranges and grapefruits attached to the crates, giving the vehicle the appearance of an innocent fruit hauler. When the truck broke down along the highway on a desolate road in Georgia, he and his partner were sure that they would be found out. As the local sheriff's vehicle slowed to see what the problem was, the two men did their best to cover their fear. Fortunately, they were able to fool the cop, who even procured a local mechanic to assist them. They were soon on their way toward Philadelphia, the sheriff none the wiser that he had just assisted the Philadelphia mafia in trafficking illegal contraband. When they reached their destination, they met the mob boss and his henchmen. The pugnacious boss informed them that he would be paying with a check. The grower tried to refuse it, stating that it was a cash-only deal. The mobster replied by showing him the butt of his pistol. "You'll take a check, or you'll take this," he said in a low voice. Forced to accept the worthless piece of paper, the disappointed grower left, wondering if he had been set up from the beginning of his dealings with the gang in Jupiter.

The land in Jupiter Farms on Italian Farms Road was later purchased by actor Burt Reynolds, who lived there for years and built a ranch on the site. "Big Al's" legendary presence on the Treasure Coast of Florida adds greatly to our colorful and controversial history.

8

The Notorious Ashley Gang

Sheriff's Deputies Barfield and Hannon walked slowly along the edge of Old Dixie Highway, both drenched in sweat from the heat of the dusty summer day. They were headed toward a small collection of homes and roadside businesses called Fruita, in tiny Gomez, Florida. Sheriff George Baker had sent them out to this bleak wilderness to make an arrest, a task that they had both met with apprehension. The reason for their anxiety was that they had heard a good deal about the suspect they were in search of. As they walked, they formulated a plan for what they would do when they confronted him. The deputies agreed that they would take the soft approach by convincing him to come along with them peacefully for some routine questioning in reference to a serious crime that had recently been committed. This was just another day on the job.

They caught the scent of burning wood and left the road, venturing into the thick pine and palmetto scrub to investigate. There was some movement from within the dense bushes, so they grew wary and drew their guns, carefully moving forward. They froze when they heard the telltale clicks of guns being cocked. Their blood ran cold when a calm voice with a thick southern drawl came from somewhere behind them. "Hold it right there, boys. Put down them rifles. Put up your hands and step in here." Terrified, the two deputies quickly dropped their weapons and followed the instructions, lowering their heads and stepping through the dense vegetation toward the voice. They entered a small clearing, where they found themselves facing two rough-looking men standing near a small

John Ashley at Raiford Prison. *Steve Carr Collection.*

campfire, each holding a pistol leveled directly at them. The two scared deputies hurriedly explained what they were there for. One of the gun-wielding assailants, a handsome man of average height with dark, wavy hair, lowered his pistol and sat down on a log, calmly turning to look at the fire. He then gave them a message for the sheriff: "Tell Baker not to send any more chicken hearted-men with rifles, or they are apt to get hurt."

The two deputies, weaponless and shaken from their encounter, headed back north to Stuart with the message. They had just been introduced to John Ashley and his very dangerous brother, Bob.

The early pioneers of the southeast coast of Florida were a tough group of individuals. Long before the advent of air conditioning, the harsh climate and inexpensive land appealed to those who wanted to make a new life for themselves. Many of them had followed the progress of Henry Flagler's railroad, establishing all the small communities along the Treasure Coast from Sebastian to Jupiter. Some were running from the law in other parts of the country, and some were just wild and adventurous. Many had come to find a warmer climate to deal with diseases, such as the dreaded consumption.

The tiny community of Salerno, located on a shallow tributary known as the Manatee Pocket, was an early center for the burgeoning commercial fishing industry. Located in the very northern region of Palm Beach County, it was a rural backwater where the families who lived and worked there struggled to make a living in the hot and humid climate, seeking out a hardscrabble existence from the land or the sea. When the railroad came through in 1893, things began to change as civilization began to take hold, but it was still a rough place located far from the county seat. The locals were suspicious of outsiders and looked out for one another. They were also mistrustful of law enforcement, so they often took things into their own hands when it became necessary. They called it the "Board of the Barrel of Correction," and it consisted of tying the offender over a large wooden barrel and thrashing him with a horsewhip.

In 1911, a family moved to the area just south of Salerno. Joe Ashley had come with his wife and children from Pompano to work on the East Coast Railroad as a wood chopper. Shortly after he arrived, he started to dabble in making bootleg whiskey. It was a hardscrabble environment for everyone, and Joe and his family became well known for their willingness to help those in need. His son John was a smart and resourceful lad who spent a lot of time in the wilderness. Like the rest of the Ashley family, John was well liked in the small community. In his travels through the woods, he began to frequent the camps of the Seminole trappers in hopes of making some money. While there, John became acquainted with a Seminole Indian named DeSoto Tiger. In December 1911, the two of them embarked on a trapping and hunting excursion in the Everglades. While there, a violent altercation took place between them, most likely alcohol induced. No one knows exactly what took place out there in the wilderness, but a short time later, John Ashley showed up to sell his furs alone. On December 29, 1911, the body of DeSoto Tiger was discovered by a dredging outfit that was digging the Fort Lauderdale canal.

John Ashley was now the suspect in a possible murder and a fugitive from the law. That was when local law enforcement sent the two deputies on their fruitless mission to pick him up for questioning. So began the reckless, lawless career of one of the most prominent criminals in Florida history.

John knew that the heat was on, so he left the state, traveling west. After some time passed, he grew homesick and returned to Florida in 1914 with the intention of surrendering to law enforcement. This time, he willingly

DeSoto Tiger, the Seminole Indian John Ashley killed. *Steve Carr Collection*.

went along with Deputy Robert Baker, giving him no trouble at all. John openly admitted to killing Tiger in the Everglades but claimed that it was in self-defense. His first trial ended in a mistrial, in which he was acquitted by a jury of his peers. It was a different era, and there was no way that the residents of the area would believe an Indian's account of the incident over

John Ashley's. Realizing this fact, the prosecuting attorney then requested a new trial in Dade County. John didn't like the sound of this at all, so when the sheriff's son, Deputy Robert Baker, took him back to the crude jail, he had a surprise in store. Deputy Baker was carrying a plate of food that John's mother had sent for him. He handed the plate to John to hold while he unlocked the jail door. Seizing the opportunity, John immediately threw the plate to the ground and bolted away, quickly scaling a fence and vanishing into the night. John Ashley had made a fool of Deputy Robert Baker, thus starting a blood feud with law enforcement that would last for many years.

BANK ROBBERS

Due to the circumstances surrounding the murder trial, John Ashley apparently made the decision that a life of crime was the best choice for him. He met three career criminals and formed his first gang. Its members included a punk bank robber from Chicago who called himself Kid Lowe, a drug addict named Clarence Middleton and Roy Matthews. They started out by attempting to rob a train, an ill-planned project that proved to be a disaster from the beginning. Their inexperience got them nothing for their efforts, and they barely escaped capture. They then robbed the Stuart Bank, a venture that was moderately more successful than the train robbery, resulting in a take of $4,500.

The newspapers, immediately leaping on this sensational story, began calling them the "Ashley Gang." Kid Lowe was apparently so angry about the low amount that they had taken that he intentionally shot John in the jaw, the bullet shattering the bone and lodging next to Ashley's eye. It was such a traumatic injury that John had to stop running and was forced to surrender to the authorities. He would lose that eye and be forced to wear a glass one for the duration of his life.

John Ashley was then taken to Miami to stand trial for the murder of DeSoto Tiger. By now, the reputation of the Ashley Gang was gaining notoriety. It was the heyday of the Chicago gangsters, so the public eagerly devoured every detail of these local bandits, hanging on every juicy detail of their activities. It was said that John was such a crack shot with a pistol that he, at thirty or forty feet, could shoot through the opening of a bottle and blow out the back of it, leaving the opening intact. Also, he could supposedly cleanly shoot the head off a quail at forty feet. It wasn't long before the

Left: Ashley Gang poster. *Steve Carr Collection*.

Below: Stuart Bank on St. Lucie Avenue, 1920s. *Steve Carr Collection*.

Ashley Gang had achieved folk hero status. Soon, John and his gang had the admiration of the public from five counties, all of whom monitored their exploits. In the lawless rural setting of Southeast Florida in the early 1900s, law enforcement was often just as corrupt as many of the criminals. It seemed that John's escapades were the topic of nearly every conversation, a fact that infuriated law enforcement, specifically Deputy Robert Baker. When his father, Sheriff George Baker, died in 1920, Robert would succeed him to become sheriff of Palm Beach County. The intensity of the blood feud grew even stronger.

BOB ASHLEY, A MAN with good intentions but not nearly as intelligent as his famous brother, traveled to Miami to break John out of prison. In a brash and reckless act of violence, he hunted down and shot John's jailer, Wilber W. Hendrickson, and started a Wild West–style shootout on the streets of the busy city. After stealing a delivery truck, Bob was confronted by Officer John Riblet, and the gun battle that ensued resulted in both his and the officer's demise. In the end, all his efforts were to no avail because brother John was acquitted of the murder charge of DeSoto Tiger with a "no prosed" verdict.

John's sweetheart Laura Upthegrove in Salerno. Note the whiskey crates behind her ready for delivery. *Steve Carr Collection*.

Apparently, the jury felt that too much time had elapsed and that there was not enough evidence to convict. They may have also wanted to avoid more violence in the streets by supporters of the notorious Ashley Gang.

After this, John Ashley was immediately taken back to Palm Beach County to stand trial for the robbery of the Stuart Bank. Happy to have escaped with his life, John pleaded guilty to this and was sentenced to seventeen years at Raiford Prison. He was very well behaved, proved to be a model prisoner and followed all the rules. His good attitude and patience paid off, and in less than two years the prison allowed him to join a road gang. This proved to be his golden opportunity, and he soon escaped from the work detail with a man named Tom Maddox. The cunning John Ashley had successfully escaped from prison a second time.

While in hiding, John would be introduced to the love of his life, Laura Upthegrove. A member of an old family that lived near Lake Okeechobee, Laura was described by a reporter as "a large woman with dark hair, a deep suntan, and wore a .38 caliber revolver strapped to her waist." Laura could spit and cuss as well as any man and had a wild, untamed nature. She quickly became infatuated with the infamous outlaw, and the two of them became romantically involved. From then on, Laura Upthegrove participated in all the Ashley Gang's activities. Her reputation grew along with theirs, and she soon became known to the masses as the "Queen of the Everglades."

BOOTLEGGERS

While he was hiding from law enforcement at the homestead in Fruita, John and a few of his family members began what would become a very profitable venture. Under the tutelage of his father, Joe, he became proficient at the manufacture of bootleg whiskey. It wasn't long until he was successfully operating three stills in the area, hiring many of the local fishermen and farmers as hands. The Ashley family was always very supportive of their neighbors, often assisting people who were struggling. John would often defend his train and bank robberies by blaming the Yankees for taking all the South's money after the Civil War. He was merely getting back at them by robbing the northern insurance companies. A huge percentage of the local population heartily agreed with him.

John and his brothers Ed and Frank also began making booze runs from West End in the Bahamas to Florida. Prohibition was strictly an American

John Ashley's sister Daisy selling booze at Fruita during happy times. *Sandra Mario Provence Collection.*

law, so the British were eager to sell any kind of booze to the Americans from the many warehouses they operated in the islands. The proximity of the Stuart Inlet to the Bahamas made this a lucrative, but often risky, business. Although it was a mere sixty- to eighty-mile run to West End or Bimini, there were still many risks involved. This became a painful reality to the family in June 1921.

John had been arrested for hauling illegal booze in Wauchula, Florida. At the police station, he was recognized by someone. When the sheriff realized his identity, John was promptly returned to Raiford Prison. While he was incarcerated, his brothers Ed and Frank got in their small rumrunner and, on a moonless night, headed out of the inlet toward the Bahamas for a pickup. When they got there, they bought $13,000 worth of booze and loaded it up. The weather turned foul, so they waited for the rest of the night. The next day, they grew impatient and left during the squall. Something must have gone wrong on the high seas for the Ashley brothers, because they were never seen again. John, still in jail, had a dream that his two brothers had been murdered. Was he correct, or were they swallowed up in a violent bout with the waves? Sadly, no one will ever know.

Despite their leader being in jail, the Ashley Gang continued their lawless ways by robbing the Stuart Bank once again. They disguised John's young nephew Hanford Mobley as a woman—complete with dress and veil. They were successful in getting the money but were forced to make a desperate escape in a stolen car. A short time later, Hanford Mobley and Clarence Middleton were apprehended in Florida and immediately thrown into jail. Roy Matthews was soon caught in Georgia. It seemed like the Ashley Gang was through.

As if following in his famous uncle John's footsteps, young Hanford Mobley broke out of the Broward County lockup, taking a recently extradited Roy Matthews with him. Incredibly, John Ashley once again escaped from a road gang at Raiford Penitentiary. It is widely believed that he may have had some assistance from inside. Reunited, the gang began their illegal activities in earnest, robbing banks, making whiskey at the stills and running illegal booze across the water of the Atlantic.

In November 1923, the Ashley Gang robbed the bank in Pompano Beach, Florida. They got away with $5,000 cash and $18,000 in securities. Shortly before the robbery, the gang commandeered a taxi for their escape. John gave a single bullet to the stunned driver of the taxi with some instructions. He told the terrified man that, when the cops arrived after the robbery, he was to give the bullet to Sheriff Robert Baker along with a message: John and

John Ashley at the beach. *Sandra Mario Provence Collection.*

his gang would be waiting for him in the Everglades. John had thrown down the gauntlet and was looking for retribution with the police.

When he received the message, Sheriff Baker flew into a violent rage and quickly organized a large posse of tough locals. He then announced publicly that if he ever killed John Ashley, he would use the criminal's glass eye as a key fob. The next morning, the army of armed riders stormed the family camp at Fruita with guns blazing. John witnessed his father take a bullet and lose his life, so he shot back, killing the sheriff's cousin, Deputy Fred Baker, and barely escaping with his life. When news of Fred Baker's killing spread, the tide quickly turned against the gang, and an angry mob of townspeople came to Fruita. They then proceeded to torch the buildings, jeering loudly as the Ashley homestead and businesses went up in flames.

It seemed that time was running out for the gang. They were now forced to rely more heavily on their whiskey running business. The one thing that John Ashley hated the most was when someone tried to cheat him. After a routine whiskey delivery from the Bahamas, he and his gang discovered that several of the jugs had no whiskey at all but were filled with water. John seethed with anger over this and plotted his revenge. The gang took to their boats, eluding law enforcement by departing from the small inlet at Hobe Sound, and made their way to Bimini. When they arrived, they robbed four different liquor warehouses for $8,000. This was marked as a crime against a sovereign nation—an act of piracy. John could now add "pirate" to his criminal résumé.

Sheriff Robert Baker was bound and determined to put the Ashley Gang out of business once and for all. He got a tip that the gang was headed north on the Dixie Highway, at that time the only main highway available. Baker sent a telegram to the Sheriff Merritt of St. Lucie County that the gang was headed their way and sent four of his deputies to assist. Merritt was

The victorious posse. *Steve Carr Collection.*

somewhat of a legend himself. John Ashley once said that the only lawman that he would never want to tangle with was Sheriff Merritt. Merritt provided two of his own deputies, creating a formidable police force. They met at the small bridge that crossed the Sebastian River and formulated their plan. Working in the darkness, the officers pulled a heavy chain across the road and hung a red lantern from its center. A short time later, two young men from Sebastian stopped their car at the chained bridge and were surprised to encounter Sheriff Merritt himself, who emerged from the darkness and told them he needed a ride to the far side. The imposing lawman then lowered the chain and jumped onto their running board. They boys did as they were told and carefully made their way across the bridge.

The Ashley Gang, not suspecting that they were found out, took their sweet time traveling north. They stopped in Fort Pierce to swagger around town, visiting a barbershop for haircuts and playing a few games of pool at the local pool hall. By the time they left, darkness had fallen. They had traveled twenty-eight miles north when they saw the red lantern ahead in the distance. When they were forced to stop, they were surprised as six lawmen leapt from the surrounding bushes and swarmed over them.

The two boys from Sebastian suspected that something was about to happen, so they turned their car around and headed back across the bridge. They were shocked when they saw who the lawmen had handcuffed by the side of the road. The notorious Ashley Gang had been caught. They hurriedly

Sebastian Bridge in the 1920s, scene of the Ashley shooting. *Steve Carr Collection.*

drove off toward town to spread the news. There is much conjecture as to what happened next. After that fateful night, the four law officers took an oath that they would stick to their story until their dying days. The truth of what happened that night on that lonely, dark bridge was unknown for a very long time. Many years later, one of the deputies present that night lay on his death bed. This is what he shared.

The Real Story

Law enforcement had been desperately trying to hunt down the Ashley Gang for a very long time. For years, they had been the laughingstock of the locals as the gang seemed to break the law at will. They knew that, given the chance, they would never again let the Ashley Gang slip from their fingers. On that cool Halloween night in 1924, their prayers were finally answered. The deputies surrounded the criminals and ordered them out of their vehicle. They separated John Ashley from the others, snapped a pair of cuffs on his wrists and ordered him to hold his hands high above his head. They told him that if he moved an inch, he would be instantly shot. The deputies were all very nervous, because John had such a fearsome reputation when it came to his dealings with the police. For whatever reason, John suddenly dropped his hands and took a short step forward. That was all it took. The deputy guarding him started shooting. The other lawmen followed suit, and the night erupted into an explosion of gunfire. When it was over, all the gang members were lying dead on the ground, still in their handcuffs. One of the officers knelt and pulled John's glass eye from its socket and pocketed it. He would later give it to Sheriff Baker. The gang members' bullet-riddled bodies were then thrown roughly into the car and hauled back to Fort Pierce, where they were laid out on the sidewalk in front of Fee's Mortuary, displayed like hunting trophies to all onlookers. People gawked in disbelief that South Florida's famous "boogie men" had finally been killed.

Aftermath

Laura Upthegrove was beside herself with grief at the loss of her true love. She moved out near Belle Glade and Canal Point, where she continued to sell bootleg whiskey for a few years until she died. Her death was ruled as a suicide. The story of her demise, as told by law enforcement, left many unanswered questions. Supposedly, in a fit of anguish, she had consumed an entire bottle of lye soap and died in excruciating pain. Many people wondered why anyone would want to end their life in this horrible fashion. Laura Upthegrove was far from your average person, but was she suicidal enough to do herself away in this grisly way? Was foul play involved? Did someone who was looking for her money commit this violent act and then make it look like a suicide? The notorious Ashley Gang was accused of

John Ashley's headstone in the family plot in Hobe Sound. *Author collection*.

robbing over forty banks in the state of Florida, but none of their money was ever located. There are all sorts of rumors and conspiracy theories about it, but no one will ever know. For this historian, John Ashley and his gang will live on forever as an irreplaceable part of the violent but wonderfully colorful history of Florida's Treasure Coast.

9

The Drug Trade on the Treasure Coast, 1960~Present

The smuggling of illicit drugs is far from a new trend on Florida's Treasure Coast. The lure of high profits and adventure is very strong, often proving irresistible to many lawbreakers. As the population of the state grows, the demand for these substances increase. The hundreds of miles of coastline make it easy to find an obscure creek or cove to conceal covert operations.

In 2012, locals found that many "square groupers" and "white lobsters," slang terms for bails of marijuana and cocaine, were washing up along the beaches of Indian River County. For days afterward, locals reported packages washing up on the beaches of four counties, from Sebastian to Jupiter Inlet. Almost five hundred pounds of drugs were eventually collected. Local law enforcement officials weren't sure of the origin of the contraband, but some officers guessed that it might have been hurriedly discarded over the side of some vessel like the cigarette boats often used in high-speed smuggling operations.

There was also speculation that the bales may have been dropped from an airplane for later pickup, but this seems unlikely due to the wide area in which they were found. Near Jupiter Inlet, three young men were fishing about eight miles from shore when they spotted a large red cooler floating in the water. When they pulled it aboard and opened it, they were shocked to find sixteen bags of pure white flake cocaine. The value of this on the street was estimated to be over $500,000. After turning in the find, the three men declined interviews due to fear of retaliation from whomever

Abandoned drug runner vessel on the rocks at Gilbert's Bar. *Michael Phillips Collection.*

the stuff originally belonged to. In another case, a local fisherman called law enforcement, reporting that he had seen several burlap sacks along the beach near highway A1A in Indian River County. At the scene, police found eight bags containing seventy-five packages of soaked marijuana. A short time later, two bales of pot weighing over fifteen pounds were found near a resort in Indian River Shores.

SMUGGLING "MARY JANE"

Marijuana, better known as cannabis or pot, is an age-old substance that has been used by humans for hundreds of years. Reports of its use date back as far as 500 BC in Asia, where it was not used for pleasure, but for medicinal purposes. Hemp was widely used for making cloth and rope, and its seeds were consumed as food. Due to its fast-growing nature and usefulness, hemp was used throughout the original European colonies as early as the 1600s. Early versions of the plant contained very little tetrahydrocannabinol (THC), the chemical responsible for marijuana's mind-altering effects. It was later that religious groups learned to cultivate the plant so that it contained higher levels. In the 1800s, cannabis was sold in some pharmacies as a treatment for stomach issues and other ailments. It was used during cholera epidemics as a medicine for the agonizing abdominal cramps caused by the disease. Scientists later found that THC could be used to treat patients with AIDS-related symptoms by reducing nausea and promoting hunger.

It is believed that pot was introduced in America after the Mexican War, when refugees from that country brought it with them and showed their northern neighbors how to smoke it. During the Great Depression of the 1930s, there was much prejudice-based suspicion of "shiftless" Mexicans and their "evil weed." The Federal Marijuana Tax Act of 1937 made marijuana illegal. The act imposed an excise tax on the sale, possession or transfer of all hemp products, effectively criminalizing all but industrial uses of the plant. In 1970, President Nixon signed the Controlled Substances Act, listing marijuana as a Schedule I drug with no medicinal benefit whatsoever, along with LSD, heroin and ecstasy.

In 1972, a report from the National Commission on Marijuana and Drug Abuse released a report titled "Marijuana: A Signal of Misunderstanding." The report recommended "partial prohibition" and lower penalties for possession of small amounts of marijuana. The Nixon administration, however, ignored the report's findings.

In the Compassionate Use Act of 1996, California became the first state to legalize marijuana for medicinal use by people with severe or chronic illnesses. In 2012, Colorado and Washington became the first states to legalize marijuana for recreational use. Washington, D.C., twenty-nine states and the U.S. territories of Guam and Puerto Rico allow the use of cannabis for limited medical purposes. As of January 2018, nine states and Washington, D.C., have legalized marijuana for recreational use. The legal status of marijuana is a subject of ongoing controversy in the United States.

Treasure Coast, Smuggler's Paradise

In the turbulent years of the 1960s and 1970s, marijuana use exploded in the United States. With this huge increase in demand for the weed, smuggling became a national pastime. The dark, uneven coastline of Florida became one of the best places to bring the drugs in, especially along the relatively undeveloped beaches of the Treasure Coast. Commercial fishermen were amazed at the profits one could reap by unloading one of the pot haulers at their docks. An enterprising man could pull in as much as $10,000 for one night's work. Law enforcement officials often took bribes to simply "stay away" from the delivery sites.

In the 1980s, running drugs from the Bahamas to Florida became a dangerous and risky sport. The tradition of smuggling had been around since the days of Prohibition, but this period produced even more violent turmoil. It was estimated that 75 percent of the nation's supply of cocaine came into Florida in the mid- to late '80s, some of it being dropped from airplanes, but most coming in by boat through the Bahamas.

The drug smugglers of that era were a swaggering, cocky mixture of professional boat and auto racers, gangsters and inexperienced adventure seekers. Completing the eighty-mile dash past patrol boats, helicopters and balloons to the American shoreline with a hold full of marijuana and cocaine became a profitable and prestigious badge of honor within their ranks. This activity resulted in almost daily periods of mayhem for the Coast Guard, often culminating in high-speed chases and gunfire. The Colombia-based drug organizations that controlled most of the world's cocaine would fly their product north and transfer it to boats, either by loading it along the docks of Bimini, Grand Bahama or other islands close to Florida. From there, the speedboats would load up and make their dangerous runs. Another technique was to drop large duffle bags from the airplanes to prearranged spots in the ocean where speedboats would pick them up. In the case of marijuana, small boats would travel offshore to meet large freighters that brought tons of the drug from locations in South America. Sometimes these rendezvous points would be discovered by authorities and the bales would be quickly discarded overboard, only to end up on the Florida shoreline as square groupers.

Smuggling in the Air

In the year 1981, Florida aviation officials reported that smugglers' planes were flying low to the ground into Florida air space in the dark without lights. This dangerous scenario caused many legitimate pilots to discontinue night flights due to fear of a collision with them. Another technique the smugglers would use was to follow in the wakes of commercial airliners, thus avoiding radar detection. Most of these planes would be deemed "un–air worthy" by inspectors and often flew within feet of the passenger planes in an attempt to fool air traffic controllers by creating only a single blip on their screens. Many of these illicit aircrafts also carried sophisticated radar-scrambling equipment to fool authorities.

The pilots themselves were often unskilled, possessing only the most rudimentary skills to fly the plane. These airplanes were disposable, often abandoned after a hasty landing in some hidden strip of field. At that time, there were nearly forty airports from Key West to Stuart, Florida, with thousands of takeoffs per day, so the smugglers had a good chance of not being detected. No one knew for sure the exact number of illegal drugs that were transported into Florida by this dangerous method, but it is estimated that the number is very high. In 1980, 290 aircraft were seized for smuggling in the United States, with 190 of them in Florida. This activity also put a strain on drug enforcement officials as they tried to chase every suspicious plane that they detected, often taking hours of costly time and fuel in the pursuit. These chases would sometimes end with a crash in the swamp with tons of illegal marijuana or cocaine burning in the night sky. Today, the drug of choice for smuggling into South Florida by plane is cocaine.

A NEVER-ENDING BATTLE

One technique that law enforcement used to monitor just how much cocaine and pot was coming into the country at any given point was to keep track of the street price. If the cost went down dramatically, it meant that demand was down and smugglers were successfully getting more drugs through the coastal blockades. The smugglers resorted to a saturation technique, releasing a barrage of sixty or seventy boats at one time from the Bahamas in the hopes of getting most of them through. If successful, they would sometimes try to elude the authorities by escaping into one of the narrow twisting tributaries of the Florida coast, leading them on a winding, raucous chase at sixty miles an hour. These encounters often ended abruptly when the speedboat would make a miscalculation on the depth of the water or take a turn too sharply, ending up with a torn hull over overturned, the pilot injured or dead.

THE BOAT BUSINESS SOARS

Since the early 1960s, Florida has been home to many famous powerboat racers, with crafts that could exceed speeds of 140 miles per hour on the open water. As the price of cocaine exploded, many of these fearless adventurers would become part-time drug runners. The boat business in South Florida experienced an immense surge in revenue, as the lure of massive profits drew many retailers into illegal partnerships with smugglers. In the late 1980s a popular boat manufacturer, Midnight Express of Opa-locka, Florida, admitted to assisting smugglers by laundering ill-gotten profits for them. They were then ordered to manufacture $500,000 worth of speedboats for the DEA to use in the war against drugs.

The battle with relentless cocaine smugglers continues. The difference is that, nowadays, federal agents utilize state-of-the-art coastal interceptor vessels that can cost up to $950,000. These forty-one-foot-long aluminum boats are outfitted with four 350-horsepower motors, are equipped with rotating night-vision cameras and can withstand the roughest of conditions on the water during any pursuit. The war on smuggling is far from lost.

Buried Treasure on the Treasure Coast

This is an interesting story that shows the level of smuggling activity in Southeast Florida. In the early 1980s, a Treasure Coast man was arrested for marijuana smuggling and money laundering. Despite vehemently pleading innocence, he was convicted of smuggling five and half tons of marijuana from Florida to Tennessee. Once considered a hero bandit by the locals, this man had been operating a successful local retail business for years. A short time after his arrest on the smuggling charge, it was discovered, in an FBI sting, that he laundered millions of dollars from his marijuana operation in Southeast Florida. The pot smuggling case got him thirteen years in prison, and the laundering case got him another ten. A couple of years later, it was discovered that he had continued to run the money laundering business through covert connections from prison and was sentenced to another three and a half years. A brash and boastful man, he told law enforcement officials that he was able to run his business so efficiently because he had bribed high-ranking local officials. This was later found to be true, and the lead investigator on the case was arrested for involvement in the illegal activity. Shortly after his parole in the late 1980s, the entrepreneur was again arrested for purchasing thirty-three pounds of cocaine from federal agents.

This man also owned a huge ranch in southeast Florida. After his arrest, the massive property was confiscated by the federal government.

The government claimed that, over the years, he had laundered millions of dollars through his marijuana smuggling business in very small bills. He bragged that he had over $40 million in assets. The FBI did locate about $2 million in overseas banks, but the rest was never found. The fact that large amounts of money were not located during this investigation led to much speculation. Inevitably, the rumor mill began to churn.

One of the popular rumors was that thieves dug a large tunnel underneath his mother's home in Fort Pierce to get at his safe, allegedly pilfering nearly $1 million from it. Based on this report that he himself filed, the agents thoroughly searched the property for the ill-gotten remains of the loot, destroying part of the house in the process. The wild talk of buried treasure soon grew.

The attention was then turned to the ranch. Tales of huge amounts of cash buried on the property began to circulate. As time passed, details were added such as a maze of intricate underground tunnels on the property where the money was hidden. Former drug dealers and fellow associates came to authorities with maps and stories of buried treasure on the property. Several people have been stopped by law enforcement with shovels and picks for digging, the property is dotted with the potholes of unsuccessful searches. There were unconfirmed stories of a buried cache of up to $500 million buried on the property near the main house. Walls have been breached and floors torn up in searches for loot. To this day, nothing has been found, so his secret stash remains unclaimed. Active searches have waned in recent years, but the legend of the smuggling treasure will live on forever.

Successful Smuggler Turned "Rat"

In 1991, another Treasure Coast man was convicted of smuggling nine tons of cocaine into the state through the Treasure Coast. He cooperated with DEA officials for seven years, eventually getting his sentence reduced to thirteen years. The information he provided led to the arrest of over one hundred people whom he worked with from the mid-1980s to the time of his arrest. Early on in his career, he established solid ties with leaders of the Colombian drug cartels that supplied much of the cocaine and marijuana to South Florida. He devised a system in which huge shipments of drugs would be loaded onto freighters on the Colombian coast and delivered to the Bahamas, where it would then be loaded onto smaller vessels for transport to the United States across the narrow channel. It was then covertly delivered to the private beachfronts of several high-end homes along the Treasure Coast, including Vero Beach, Melbourne and Fort Pierce. It would then be shipped to California, Michigan, Colorado, Idaho, Washington, Oregon and Georgia.

In his damning testimony, he recounted tales of dealing with corrupt Bahamian officials, Colombian drug lords and even a South American billionaire. By use of his testimony, agents were also able to uncover a system of supplying drugs to inmates in the Miami Dade Correctional Facility. This man's testimony led to the arrests of those responsible for the smuggling of two hundred tons of marijuana, sixteen tons of cocaine and between $7 and $15 million in confiscated equipment. This case uncovered the high level of activity of drug smuggling along the beautiful Treasure Coast of Florida.

A Fisherman's Brush with the Law

Growing up along the Treasure Coast, many locals were witnesses to illicit activity. The following is a true story told by Ken Cook, a local businessman and fisherman who resides in Vero Beach, Florida:

Growing up on the treasure coast, I spent a lot of time on the water fishing. As I got older, I started commercial fishing for kingfish. Making a living as a commercial king fisherman means long, hard hours spent at sea, with most of those hours occurring after dark when the best bite happens. Being a part of the commercial fishing business back in the '70s also put me in the middle of the "square grouper" bite. "Square grouper" was the term coined for floating bails of pot that were typically dropped from larger ships onto smaller, faster "runner" boats. "Square groupers" were often dropped overboard from larger ships when they were being chased by coast guard.

In the 1970s, when fishing off the Treasure Coast of Florida, you either saw "square groupers," caught a few or knew someone who did. Because the commercial fishermen were a relatively small community, word spread fast when the "groupers" were being caught and who was catching them. Not all, but certainly some, commercial fisherman used this as a way support their fishing habit. A good night's king fishing might bring $700 to $1,000. Add a square grouper to your catch, make a quick sale, and you've added another $2,000 to $2,500 to your haul. One can certainly understand the temptation of this activity!

Early on, the talk was about one guy or another who found one or two bails, and you would see new fishing gear or motors on their boats the next time you saw them. The rumors seemed to be substantiated with the spending, especially when they would "flash the cash." As time went on, good people would sometimes find themselves doing bad things. In fact, several fishermen I knew switched their focus from fishing for kings to running for smugglers. I have to admit, it wasn't easy seeing the new trucks that had been "tricked out," boats with two, then three outboards, and hearing about all the cash these guys were spending around town.

The only thing that kept me from joining in was the fact that "running" for smugglers was illegal; therefore, being a runner made you the smuggler. Also, if I knew what these guys were doing, then certainly the people in drug enforcement had to know. I guess I just didn't want to be caught. As time went on more and more people joined in the group. It was general knowledge at the time that merely being a well-known fisherman kept you "under the radar" of the DEA. For a while it seemed that no one was getting caught. It turned out that the guys in charge of drug enforcement were only building their cases against everyone involved. All they had to do was find a fisherman, most of them in their early twenties, with a nice truck and boat, and bingo! You have a runner. There was just no way a king fisherman could make enough money to buy these toys. When the "hammer dropped," they started picking up guys one after another. Most of the time they caught them "in the act," with the bails onboard their vessel.

I fished, from time to time, on my brother Johnny's boat. It was a new twenty-four-foot Beehive with inboard diesel with a value of around $35,000 (a lot of money in the late '70s). Johnny also drove a new Ford 150, a two-toned 4x4 that was lifted with bull-bars, big tires and rims. He was twenty-two years old and had a truck-boat package that placed him smack in the middle of the DEA's radar. What they didn't know was that Johnny was a straight shooter who wasn't about to run drugs for money. He just wasn't that kind of guy. He had our mother, who lent him the money for the toys.

I was lucky enough to be fishing with him on the very night the DEA was planning a drug bust on Johnny. We pulled into the dock around 1:00 a.m. with a load of kingfish and were in the process of tying off when I immediately noticed three or four guys spread around the area. I grew a little apprehensive because I knew that, at this time of the morning, if you *see guys, you know they are not just "standing around." We all knew that something was going on, but never dreamed that it would have something to do with us, so we just went about our business of getting the boat on the trailer and going home. Johnny stepped onto the dock and headed to the truck. I think he made four or five steps and the place lit up. Suddenly there were bright lights shining on us and three or four guys headed towards us yelling "hands up—put your hands up!"*

We all froze; our hands in the air. As I gradually realized who the men were and what was happening, I could not help but laugh at the wasted effort of all these people and their focus on, of all people, my brother. I knew the kind of man Johnny was, and that they wouldn't even find a normal cigarette on his boat, let alone pot. They pulled us out of the boat at gun point, patted us down for weapons, and proceeded to search Johnny's boat and truck over the next two to three hours looking for drugs. During the search, they informed us that there was no way someone his age could afford such a nice boat and truck as a fisherman. For the agents, the experience proved to be uneventful, because there were no drugs to be found.

In the end, they arrested close to a dozen fisherman I personally knew. All went to jail; some for longer than others. Some of them did "hard time" until, as the rumors have it, they gave up names and contacts. The ones who got away with it stopped after the big bust. Some of these guys were still spending hundred-dollar bills dated from the '70s, even after Y2K. The lesson we all learned was that running drugs is like gambling—there are no winners.

10

Pirates and Smugglers of the Treasure Coast Today

I t is a beautiful but blisteringly hot day in Fort Pierce, Florida, at the annual Treasure Coast Pirate Festival. Every year in late February, dozens of weekend pirates descend on Veterans Memorial Park to meet and greet one another and celebrate the memory of another world from long ago, each of them presenting their personal interpretation of history to hundreds of people. There are pirate presentations, cannon firing demonstrations, children's events and dozens of vendors selling everything from eyepatches to wooden and plastic swords. The pirate reenactors go to extreme lengths to remain authentic to the genre, meticulously preparing their buccaneer gear down to the last button. At times, one feels that he or she has been transported back in time to New Providence Island in the year 1715. Raucous music is always playing, and rollicking pirates roam the trails, ready to answer any questions about the subject they love dearly.

Why the fascination with piracy? It may be that, throughout history, these rogues have been admired and revered as folk heroes by those of us who often feel stilted and confined by our regimented existence. Legions of devoted fans seem to have a vision of the Caribbean pirates as swarthy swashbuckling warriors who preyed on victims who, most of the time, deserved what they got. Many of us have seen the film *Captain Blood*, starring Errol Flynn, in which he portrays a dashingly handsome, swaggering pirate captain. In the film, Dr. Peter Blood was a true gentleman who was forced by outside circumstances to become a feared buccaneer.

Above: Errol Flynn as Captain Blood, circa 1935. *Public domain.*

Left: *Treasure Island* cover. *Charles Scribner's Sons, 1911.*

TREASURE ISLAND

Robert Louis Stevenson was responsible for a huge surge in interest and popularity in the subject. His book *Treasure Island* was an adventure of epic success and provided us with many of the images of the pirate that we have today. The truth behind this wonderful work is that Stevenson was thirty years old when he wrote most of it in the mountains of Scotland. The rest of the book was written in Switzerland, with his family all around him. He even had input for the storyline from his young son and other family members.

Though not a success when it was originally released in *Young Folks* magazine, it became popular when released as a book. The impact of this work cannot be underestimated in our modern view of piracy. Its descriptive prose introduced us to maps, crosses, one-legged pirates, buried treasure and parrots on the shoulder. A boy's adventure, it has stood the test of time.

The Disney company is responsible for the recent surge in popularity of the genre with its wildly popular Pirates of the Caribbean series. What child doesn't love Captain Jack Sparrow?

THE REAL PIRATES OF THE CARIBBEAN

History is often viewed through rose-colored glasses. The harsh reality is that most real pirates were far from the swashbuckling, colorfully adorned brigands that we have come to know. Think of how the Somali pirates are viewed by society today. They are vilified as the essence of evil corruption and feared by all mariners who sail too close to their home shores. The average American feels that they should all be imprisoned or killed for their crimes. This is the same way the original Caribbean pirates were viewed by the civilized world in the seventeenth and eighteenth centuries. They were loathed as the lowest of the low—a primitive lot of subhuman marauders. Maritime travelers were terrified at the prospect of being attacked by them.

In the late seventeenth century, Captain Henry Morgan and his rabble of pirates were quickly approaching the undefended city of Panama, waving their cutlasses, spreading through the thick, steamy, insect-ridden jungle like a disease. They were so poorly provisioned that they killed and

Ye Crew's New Roger. *Sketch by Don Maitz.*

devoured anything living for sustenance. As the panic-stricken citizens of the city waited for the invasion of the impending mob, they experienced the very real fear that they might *actually be eaten* by the starving pirates. They were also well aware of Morgan's reputation for cruelty. Those who survived the onslaught would be mercilessly tortured to reveal information

"The Fight." *Sketch by Don Maitz.*

about any hidden valuables they might know of. It is hard to imagine the level of fear that they experienced in those hours as these people awaited Morgan's attack.

There were many different types of men who turned to a life of crime on the high seas. A vast majority of them were filthy, uneducated and unemployed sailors with no prospects who owned no more than the shirts on their backs. More than a few were outright bloodthirsty criminals with very little moral character who would kill a man in cold blood for the smallest pittance. Some were reluctant crew members of prize ships who were pressed into the life against their will because they possessed valuable skills such as carpentry or medical knowledge. Theirs was a sullen, lonely existence that often dragged on for years.

Then there were the captains and leaders of the pirate operations. I have always been in awe of these characters and highly respect what they accomplished in their short careers. These men were, for the most part, experienced seamen who had to be smart and proficient at everything they did. The typical pirate captain had to know the intricate workings of a seventeenth-century sailing ship and what purpose each of its hundreds of coiled ropes, deadeyes and sails served in all sorts of weather conditions. He had to be a natural leader who understood the nuances of differing personalities and could motivate men to follow him. He had to be prepared to deal with the constant threat of fighting and mutiny aboard ship and what the proper punishments should be for violations of the rules. The close quarters of a seventeenth-century ship would have made these skills essential to his survival.

During regular day-to-day operations, the captain was just like a common sailor, taking part in all the same work as everyone else aboard ship. The minute a prize ship was sighted, the captain assumed his leadership role, and his commands were to be followed without question. A pirate captain was voted in democratically and could be voted out by a disgruntled crew. Just ask Captain Charles Vane, who was set adrift in a small boat after being accused of cowardice by his crew.

Back to the Treasure Coast Pirate Festival. My wife, Tricia, and I have participated for several years now and have gotten to know some of the people who make events like this tick. We would like to introduce you to a few of them who intrigued us the most.

CAPTAIN BOB

Captain Bob is one who has the definite look and attitude of the original buccaneer. He saunters around the paths with a swagger and a wide smile that reminds one of the free spirits who reigned over the seas hundreds

Captain Bob
takes aim with
his flintlock.
*Courtesy of
Captain Bob.*

of years ago. He and his faithful better half, Flintlock Fannie, are rarely seen apart. Originally from Pittsburgh, Pennsylvania, Bob has always had a great appreciation of history, especially the period known as the Golden Age of Piracy.

Captain Bob and Flintlock Fannie were always fans of Renaissance festivals and together experienced the urge to participate. In the year 2000, they got the idea to dress in character and tour daycare centers to entertain children while teaching them about an important part of history. Since then they have visited and participated in countless pirate festivals from Pittsburgh to Nassau in the Bahamas. He cuts a compelling figure as a seventeenth-century buccaneer with his flawless period frocks and his trademark eight silver skull rings.

BLACKBEARD LIVES

Captain Edward Teach, better known as Blackbeard. *Courtesy of Jim Laird, 2019.*

Blackbeard and Crazy Sadie are impossible to miss at any of the local pirate festivals. Jim Laird is Blackbeard, the most famous pirate of them all, and his wife, Donna, is his "pirate lass, Crazy Sadie," always at his side. She has a little rhyme that she likes to recite to let people know what they would be up against if they cross her: "Even though you be dead, you don't get to keep yer head—Crazy Sadie be about—she'll cut yer head off and hang it from 'er bowsprit."

Blackbeard's charisma and appearance are so remarkable that he makes the festivals better just by making an appearance. He is tall, rangy, boisterous and charismatic with a long black beard and ready smile. It's easy for one to believe that the actual Blackbeard was much like Jim, or vice versa. Natural entertainers, Jim and Donna have built a business on being "all things pirate." At the festivals, they have a booth that sells pirate swords, mugs, knives, banners and anything else to help you "be the pirate you want to be." Jim also does a Blackbeard show several times a day, making hundreds of children shriek with laughter at his antics. He is an expert on pirate history and a burgeoning author, having recently finished writing a book titled *Edward Teach—Better Known as Blackbeard*.

A machinist by trade, Jim got into the pirate business on a dare and proved to be such a natural at it that it became a way of life for him and his wife. Eighteen years ago, he was asked to portray the infamous pirate at an event held at the Burt Reynolds Theater in Jupiter, Florida. It was an announcement of the important archaeological discovery of Blackbeard's ship, the *Queen Anne's Revenge*, by Jupiter resident Captain Mike Daniels. There were other pirate reenactors present, but Jim was such a natural that he stole the show. The rest is history for them. Together, he and Donna travel to pirate festivals, Renaissance fairs and countless private parties, performing in character and having fun while teaching about history. It's comforting to know that the pirate Blackbeard still lives among us on the Treasure Coast of Florida.

Jim "Blackbeard" Laird. *Courtesy of Jim Laird.*

CAPTAIN DAN LEEWARD AND HOLLY ROGER

Captain Dan Leeward and Holly Roger are members of the Pirates of the Treasure Coast, a loose association of pirate reenactors who go to great pains to be historically accurate in everything they do. They have been members of the organization since its inception in 2010. Their appearance shows their level of dedication. Dan, with his flowing gray beard and small, round spectacles, is the quintessential pirate—all the way from his rope sandals to his weathered tricorn hat. An excellent carpenter by trade, Dan built his own pirate ship on wheels that he pulls to the festivals for children to play on and get pictures. He is also a craftsman with canvas, working with a vintage one-hundred-year-old sewing machine. He and Holly both have a real appreciation for "the old ways." They started their pirate careers in the year 2010 at the Peanut Island Pirate Invasion in Palm Beach County, Florida. Since then, they have attended dozens of festivals over the years. We asked Dan how he got his name: Captain Dan Leeward.

"Well," he says, scratching his beard, "when we were on the pirate ship at the Peanut Island Pirate Invasion, I realized that I had to go to the bathroom. Being inexperienced at the time, I went to the side of the ship and began to do my business. I quickly realized that the breeze was in my face, and that I was getting drenched with my own urine. It was then that I heard the laughs and catcalls of the experienced pirates. 'Leeward!' they shouted repeatedly, meaning that I needed to go to the opposite side of the boat where the wind was blowing out to sea. Well, the name just stuck."

Holly, who is also a musician, keeps an array of crude instruments with her for children to play. She believes in education through mediums such as song and drama. She loves to entertain young people during the festivals.

Holly is a healer with a doctor of naturopathy degree from Trinity School of Natural Health and uses homeopathic remedies. She is an artist and did all the artwork on the pirate ship and is also a talented set designer with a keen interest in history, music, and rescuing animals. They are both pirate "purists"—braving the elements for days during the festivals in their canvas tents with no modern amenities, rain or shine.

"Being a pirate lets me be bad for a while," Holly says. "I am normally a very strait-laced person."

Both enjoy the common interests and sense of comradery that they feel with other reenactors at the festivals. "Our favorite time," she continues, "is

Captain Dan Leeward and Holly Roger. *Authors' collection.*

when all of the people go home after the festival closes. That's when the fun starts. Everyone has a little rum, share laughs, and do what pirates do. That is when the real pirates come out."

Dan's interest in the pirate lifestyle started later in life, but Holly's occurred much earlier. Growing up in the maritime Tidewater area in Hampton–Newport News, Virginia, she remembers attending an event called the Blackbeard Fest with her family as a child. The performers there had such a profound effect on her that it changed her life.

The couple has such a passion for portraying the history of the Caribbean buccaneers that they have carried their knowledge into the school system. A good friend of theirs, Robin Stern, is a teacher at a local middle school. She is also a pirate who calls herself "the Governess." Four times a year, Dan and Holly visit her classroom and put on a Pirate Party for the class of students that wins a quarterly contest. Staying completely in character the entire time, they regale the students with stories, songs and explanations of how the pirates lived. Holly wants to emphasize the fact that they were not all homicidal monsters but real people who had to survive in an incredibly difficult environment.

"The kids love it," Holly states. "We end every pirate session by singing a nontraditional song called 'Mariner's Revenge.'"

Captain Dan Leeward and Holly Roger are true pirates of the Treasure Coast.

DON MAITZ

Another fascinating participant in the pirate festivals on the Treasure Coast is the renowned artist Don Maitz. Several of his sketches appear in this book. During the festivals, Don can be found working diligently at his easel, chatting with anyone who passes by and expresses interest in his work. He is an expert on buccaneer history and loves to talk about the subject at length. A few minutes with Don, and it becomes evident to the listener that he is an extremely knowledgeable pirate enthusiast. His presence is a welcome addition to any gathering.

"Foulbottom." *Sketch by Don Maitz.*

Maitz's history is a quite impressive one. He has been painting professionally since graduation from the Paier School of Art in 1975. He's produced over two hundred book covers of fantastic subjects and has illustrated works of authors such as Stephen King, Ray Bradbury, Isaac Asimov and George R.R. Martin. He was a concept artist for the animated feature films *Jimmy Neutron Boy Genius* and *Ant Bully*.

Maitz originated the iconic Captain Morgan Original Spiced Rum character and provided paintings for ad campaigns when the product was owned by Seagrams & Sons. Maitz has been commissioned by the National Geographic Society and most New York publishing houses. The History Channel and various news programing have featured his art in their broadcasts, and the Odyssey Marine Exploration included his art in its nationally touring exhibits.

Pirate Treasure: A Shipwreck Museum recently opened in St. Thomas in the American Virgin Islands with his art displayed.

Maitz's work has been a favorite installment in public exhibitions across the United States with many museum exhibitions. He received a Silver Medal from the Society of Illustrators, two Hugo awards for Best Artist, a Howard Award, an Inkpot award (from the San Diego Comic Con), Ten Chesley Awards and an Award of Excellence at the 24th International Marine Exhibition at the Maritime Gallery at Mystic Seaport. His works are in two museum collections and numerous private homes.

Don lives in Florida with his wife, Janny Wurts, a noted author of twenty published books and thirty-five short stories of fantastic literature. She is an accomplished artist and paints the covers to her novels. She is published by HarperCollins, UK. Their website is www.paravia.com.

As you can see, Don Maitz is one of the more well-known pirates of the Treasure Coast.

Captain Fizz

I cannot give an accurate account of maritime history on the Treasure Coast of Florida without mentioning another featured guest at the local pirate festivals. He is world-famous treasure hunter Captain Carl Fismer. Even though Carl is about as close to a living legend as you can get, when you meet him in person, you will not find a friendlier, more down-to-earth person. He loves to talk to people, and is a master storyteller, as evidenced in his book, *Uncharted Waters: The Life and Times of Captain Fizz*. With over thirty years of treasure search and salvage experience, he is one of the most respected and knowledgeable diving professionals in the world.

Over his long career, Carl has worked with some of the leaders in treasure hunting, including respected treasure historian Jack Haskins and Mel Fisher on the Atocha. He has worked extensively on the 1715 wrecks on the Treasure Coast and is an expert on the region's history. His area of expertise is shipwrecks—especially Spanish shipwrecks. He has worked over three hundred shipwrecks in the United States, Bahamas, Dominican Republic, Jamaica, the Indian Ocean and Central and South America, successfully recovering millions of dollars in Spanish gold, silver, jewels and other artifacts. "Fizz," as he is known to friends, directed part of the salvage diving of the *Santa Margarita*, sister ship to the *Nuestra Senora de Atocha*, which was discovered by Mel Fisher. In 1986, he led an expedition to the Silver Shoals in the Dominican Republic, where he located the famed galleon *Concepción*, which sank during a hurricane in 1641. In 1992, he traveled to Sri Lanka and dove with Sir Arthur C. Clarke of *2001: A Space Odyssey* fame, in association with the Great Basses Reef Treasures. Carl's reputation is so well known that he has appeared on the television show *Pawn Stars* four times as the designated expert of antiquities.

In May 2010, Captain Fismer was awarded the Mel Fisher Lifetime Achievement Award for perseverance in following his quest for life, his motivation of mankind in the search for knowledge, discovery and the ambitions of the human spirit and the ability to achieve in life what others might only dare to dream.

CAPTAIN HONEY BADGER

The thunderous boom is so loud that every one of the thousands of festival attendees pauses and turns toward the direction from which it came. One of the most authentic and exciting parts of the show is the firing of the cannons out over the Indian River. Several times a day, the roaring fire of the guns is heard for miles in every direction. The man largely responsible for this bit of mayhem is Dustin Tucker. Ever since joining the ranks of the Pirates of the Treasure Coast (POTTC), he has been known as the cannoneer Captain Honey Badger. One of the most well-known of the pirates, the captain takes his work and duties very seriously indeed.

Always a fan of Renaissance festivals and medieval fairs, Dustin made the move to full-blown piracy about seventeen years ago. At one of these gatherings, he met a fellow pirate reenactor in full dress. Dustin was so impressed with both the attire and the pirate attitude he went out and purchased his first period clothes and showed up ready for action the very next day. From an early age, Dustin has always held a keen interest in weaponry and firepower, so he began to study the military history of the Golden Age of Piracy. In his travels, he was thrilled to find and procure some weapons: beautiful French 1733 flintlock pistols. From there, he began to collect cannons, knives and other custom arms. Along with the growth of his knowledge about the military tactics and weapons of yesterday came the desire to share his knowledge through teaching and live demonstration. With his keen intellect and penchant for the dramatic, Captain Honey Badger soon became the head cannoneer for the POTTC.

Dustin is a specialist on dealing safely and effectively with ancient weapons. Also, he has always been aware of the many dangers involved with live cannon firing demonstrations. He has strict rules of conduct when firing and takes great pains to use all the safety protocol necessary to keep everyone safe during the shows. "It takes the power of two sticks of dynamite to send a cannonball effectively at a target," Dustin says. "I will not fire unless all civilians are a safe distance away."

Safety is of the highest priority to him, which is why Captain Honey Badger has never lost a man or had any injuries at any of his engagements. He uses a cannon with a Spanish carriage and an English barrel and always utilizes the proper amount of black powder to give a thunderous boom. He shares that, in the days of the pirates, any ratio of powder to the bore diameter was used to get the job done.

Make sure you catch Captain Honey Badger demonstrate his fine trade at the next pirate festival. As a testament to his heavy emphasis on safety during his shows, he says, "At what other event do you yell at children, make them cry, and have their parents applaud?"

COMMODORE CUTTER

If you attend any of the pirate festivals on the Treasure Coast, you will most likely encounter a distinguished-looking buccaneer at the front gate with a goatee and spectacles. He can be seen at almost any time directing traffic, setting up displays or helping vendors with any number of issues. On the rare occasion when he can relax, he settles into his pirate persona, hanging out with the other buccaneers, playing his fiddle or guitar and spending time with his like-minded associates. His "civilian" name is Stephen Goff, but everyone in the festival world knows him as Commodore Cutter, or "Cutter" for short.

Cutter is a surprisingly eloquent pirate, who is also a talented musician, tradesman and student of history. He became interested in the subject of piracy at the age of eight. His father, also a musician, was playing a popular song on his guitar. As young Stephen listened, he became fascinated with the lyrics. The song was "A Pirate Looks at Forty," by Jimmy Buffet. He realized how much his father loved the song, so he loved it as well. As he listened to the hard-luck story of Buffet's buccaneer, he knew what he wanted to be when he grew up.

As he grew older, he pushed this dream back to pursue a career that society would view as more realistic and would pay the bills. He learned how to use his skilled hands in a trade, spending twenty years working for an automotive clutch manufacturer. He then switched careers, working in glass factory for a time. All the while, his childhood dream lay in the back of his mind. In the year 2003, Stephen attended a festival in his hometown of Fort Myers, Florida, called Lee Island Days. There he met some people who were dressed as pirates, and his interest was sparked. After getting to know some of these eclectic people, he decided to give the pirate lifestyle a try. Within a short time, he had purchased his first period outfit and was performing regularly at the festivals. As Stephen performed in many more events, he began to develop his own persona, and Commodore Cutter was born. He moved to Key West, Florida, and spent time as a crew member on a replica pirate ship, working as a pirate reenactor at festivals such as the Fort Taylor Pirate Festival. After about four months, he moved back to Fort Myers and got a job with Pirates of the Treasure Coast. He has been there ever since, fulfilling his childhood dream.

With so many talented and passionate people participating in these events, it's easy to see why there is so much interest in the subject of piracy, especially here on Florida's Treasure Coast.

conclusion

We residents of Florida's Treasure Coast are very proud of our colorful history. We believe that there is a little pirate in all of us. Haven't we all, at one time or another during our lives, longed to go on a pirate or smuggling adventure to an unknown destination? The freedom of the high seas beckons to us all, to a place where we can make our own rules and run our pirate kingdom our way, and by our rules.

Throughout history, both pirates and smugglers have always been admired for their daring exploits, despite the illegality of their acts. This was as true during the Golden Age of Piracy as it was during Prohibition in the 1920s. The laws were so unpopular that many buccaneers and booze smugglers were revered as heroes. No one ever remembers the pirate hunters or law enforcement officers who bravely tried to do what they thought was the right thing. It may be that we all, to a certain degree, have an instinct to resent authority, especially when someone makes a law or rule that we don't agree with. It seems that our society has always been enamored with individuals who bravely flout authority at great risk of injury or death to themselves. From time to time, we all wish that we could "stick it" to officials, especially when we believe that we have been treated unfairly, or that the rules are unjust. We all love stories of the Golden Age of Piracy, the exploits of the famous rumrunners and even the daring marijuana smugglers of the 1960s and '70s. The passage of time always heals the wounds, so we tend to forget their crimes. We only remember the brave, reckless way they were, and the risks they took will always be the stuff of legends.

We must also see their dark side. For centuries, innocent people were unjustly brutalized by violent acts perpetrated by criminals on the high seas. Even today, horrific acts of piracy regularly occur. We want to thank the thousands of people of the U.S. Coast Guard, Border Patrol and all other agencies for their brave work in fighting these scourges.

Bibliography

Carrier, Toni. "Trade and Plunder Networks in the Second Seminole War in Florida, 1835–1842." Thesis, University of Florida, 2005.

Cordingly, David. *Under the Black Flag: The Romance and the Reality of Life Among the Pirates*. Boston: Harcourt Brace & Company, 1995.

Davidsson, Robert I. "Civil War Blockade-Running at Jupiter Inlet:1861–1865." Origins and History of the Palm Beaches. May 29, 2015. pbchistory.blogspot.com.

Defoe, Daniel (Captain Charles Johnson). *A General History of the Pyrates*. Edited by Manuel Schonhorn. Mineola, NY: Dover Publications, 1999.

Ferdinando, Peter. "'Notorious and Publicly Known': Pedro Menéndez and the Indians of South Florida, 1565–1574." SISC Conference, 2012.

Greenlee, Will. "High Tech Boats Help Feds Stop Crime Locally." *Stuart News*, August 19, 2019.

Gulliver, Lemuel. *Trial of the Twelve Spanish Pirates of the Schooner Panda, a Guinea Slaver*. Cambridge, MA: Harvard University, 1834.

Hutchinson, Janet. *History of Martin County*. Stuart, FL: Martin County Historical Society, 1975.

Knetsch, Joe. *Florida's Seminole Wars, 1817–1858*. Charleston, SC: Arcadia Publishing, 2003.

Lyon, Eugene. *The Enterprise of Florida: Pedro Menéndez de Avilés and the Spanish Conquest of 1565–1568*. Gainesville: University Press of Florida, 1976.

Milanich, Jerald T. *Florida's Indians—From Ancient Times to the Present*. Gainesville: University Press of Florida, 1998.

Motte, Jacob Rhett. *Journey into the Wilderness*. Gainesville: University of Florida Press, 1963.

Procyk, Richard. "Prohibition in Jupiter." *Town of Jupiter History*, December 3, 2005.

Snyder, James D. "Jupiter Lighthouse: A Foothold on the South Florida Frontier." *Keeper's Log* (Fall 2006).

———. *A Light in the Wilderness: The Story of Jupiter Inlet Lighthouse & Southeast Florida Frontier*. Jupiter, FL: Pharos Books, 2006.

Van De Water, Frederick Franklin. *The Real McCoy*. Mystic, CT: Flat Hammock Press, 2006.

Wagner, Kip. *Pieces of Eight: Recovering the Riches of a Lost Spanish Treasure Fleet*. Port Salerno: Florida Classics Library, 1998.

Willebrandt, Mabel Walker. *The Inside of Prohibition*. Indianapolis, IN: Bobbs-Merrill Company, 1929.

Williams, Ada Coates. *Florida's Ashley Gang*. Port Salerno: Florida Classics Library, 1996.

Wilson, David. "The 1715 Plate Fleet and the Rise of the Pirates." History Today, July 30, 2015. historytoday.com.

Woodard, Colin. "Blackbeard's Final Days." *Smithsonian* (February 2014).

———. *The Republic of Pirates: Being the True and Surprising Story of the Caribbean Pirates and the Man Who Brought Them Down*. Boston: Mariner Books, 2008.

Zimmerman, Stan. *A History of Smuggling in Florida*. Charleston, SC: The History Press, 2006.